CO

CONFLUENCES

FORGOTTEN HISTORIES FROM EAST AND WEST

Ilija Trojanow/Ranjit Hoskoté

YODAPRESS

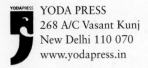

YODA PRESS
268 A/C Vasant Kunj
New Delhi 110 070
www.yodapress.in

First published in German in 2007 as *Kampfabsage* (Munich: Blessing Verlag)
First published in English in 2012 by YODA PRESS
Second impression 2013

ISBN 978-81-906186-7-0

For sale only in India, Pakistan, Bangladesh, Myanmar, Bhutan, Nepal
and Sri Lanka

Editors in charge: Arpita Das, Nishtha Vadehra
Typeset in Sabon 10.5/14
By Jojy Philip, New Delhi 110 015
Printed at Saurabh Printers Pvt Ltd, New Delhi 110 020
Published by Arpita Das for YODA PRESS

To the Inhabitants of the In-between

... we should remember that it is the 'inter'—the cutting edge of translation and negotiation, the *in-between* space—that carries the burden of the meaning of culture.

Homi K. Bhabha
The Location of Culture (1994)

Contents

No Confluence, No Culture!

Every Saturday and Sunday, all over Europe, people from different walks of life come together to support and celebrate their very own. They flock into the arenas, wearing the shirts of their heroes, eager to scream and shout for the better part of two hours. What do they sing in moments of joy and ecstasy? Which slogan unites them all, whether they are comfortably seated in Munich or quivering on their feet in Manchester? *Olé!* Rhythmically repeated in a distinct, well-known cascade: *olé ... olé olé olé*. Probably most fans link this slogan with Spain. They associate it with toreros or with Don Juan. But how many of the hooligans that whip themselves into frenzy with unrelenting *olés* realise that they are actually repeating the Arab word for God? Time and again, every Saturday and Sunday, the soccer stadiums in Europe resonate with shouts of 'Allah'!

That cry gives the lie to those ideologues of purity who believe that societies can only function when they boast of a homogeneous, home-grown culture that has developed from the core of a certain nation: one tradition, one religion, one people. They define difference as static and unbridgeable.

They are oblivious to the concealed entanglements of ancestry and the local variations of transcontinental narratives. Theirs is a flawed conviction, for it is blind to history. Take for example the claim that the West is distinguished by its enlightened Judaeo-Christian tradition (a paradox in itself, given the sharp differences between the two components of this tradition). Conventional wisdom has it that the greatness of modern Europe was established during the Renaissance, a period of enormous cultural flowering that was inspired by the idea of the individual and the rediscovery of Ancient Greece. The Renaissance is the colossal achievement of European genius and the foundation of contemporary European identity. The philosophical upheavals that led to rationality and the Enlightenment, to the division of Church and State, to Human Rights and the Idea of Freedom were provoked by the great minds of this epoch. This established narrative is neat and thoroughly lopsided.

In Chapter II (The Making of Europe) we will show that core Western values, technologies and cultural expressions were decisively formed in the cradle of the confluential Mediterranean between the 9th and the 15th centuries, with the principalities of al-Andalus, the elegantly Arabised Norman kingdom of Sicily and later on the mercantile centres of the Italian city-states, with Venice as Europe's most cosmopolitan capital, as its key points. Here accounting and cartography, philosophy and medicine, poetry and logic all flowered under both Islamic and Christian patronage. This vibrant culture of debate embraced scholars working in Granada, Baghdad, Palermo, Damascus, Bologna, Paris, Venice and Cairo. Ibn Sina (Avicenna), for example, produced an Aristotelian defence of independent inquiry and scientific truth in the 11th century. Al-Ghazali (Algazel) opposed him vehemently, claiming that the tolerant God of the philosophers could not be the God of Islam. Ibn Rushd (Averroes) countered by demonstrating Al-Ghazali's logical incoherence, upheld the autonomy of critical rational thought, and refuted the notion that faith had a monopoly on truth. Averroes became a hero and guide to many Parisian scholars, including early intellectual giants like Pierre Abelard, Roger Bacon and Albertus Magnus. They annotated his Aristotelian commentaries and deployed his ideas against a Church that was suspicious of free thought and ruthless in its suppression of heresy.

From a long-term perspective, it is clear that Arab Muslim thinkers inspired the eventual victory of critical rationalism over fundamentalist bigotry. Ibn Sina and Ibn Rushd, together with Aristotle and Plato, gave independent minds in Christendom the intellectual equipment and moral inspiration to oppose the suffocating orthodoxy of the Church, a liberating movement that led to the Renaissance.

We will trace a number of such cultural confluences that manifested themselves sometimes in an adaptation of form, sometimes in a retelling of content and sometimes in both, as shown by the example of the Sanskrit story-collection *Panchatantra*, which travelled through the *Thousand and One Nights* and Petrus Alfonsi's *Disciplina Clericalis* to Chaucer's *Canterbury Tales* and Boccaccio's *Decameron*, or by the incarnation of the Arab *muwashshaha* in the songs of the Troubadours, the very beginning of modern Western poetry. These are just two of the many examples that we will present to prove that the values and cultural achievements of the West are the result of awakenings and rebellions made possible by what we today regard as non-European sources.

&

The greatest rivers bear the most misleading names. The canon of geography dictates that the source furthest away from the mouth is the river's point of origin, and the entire watercourse takes on a single name. But no great river would reach the ocean without being fed by tributaries: the brooks, streams and rivulets that join its flow, often bringing with them more water, alluvium, minerals or fish than the source stream. By the time the great river has reached the ocean, the source is no more than a faint memory; the flow has been defined by a series of confluences along the way. But the river's official name conceals the truth of its composition; while the nametag passes into legend and lexicon, the ancestry of confluences becomes invisible. To understand the true identity of the river, we would have to pinpoint the occasions of confluence, examine the dynamics of addition and innovation played out at the merging of the waters.

Our history, regulated by concepts of singularity and pure origin, is as much of a cartographer's invention as the great river. By taking a certain tableau of it to represent a culture's form and essence, it mistakes a snapshot of the river for its whole course. By the time cultural achievements become sufficiently established in public consciousness as to be taught in school, the turmoil of their evolution has been forgotten. The confluences of every culture are concealed, and homogenising foundational myths are installed in their place. Instead of the many pasts that have produced our present, we put on the dark glasses of amnesia and see a

— SINGULARISING PAST —

singular past. The timeless stability of our culture guarantees the security of our identity. Therefore, we have to preserve the purity of our culture against contamination by the Other. By a circular argument in which the contemporary political purpose shapes its own background, this singular Past is established as testament to the uniqueness and superiority of a particular culture or nation. Although globalisation is currently depicted as a celebration of diversity, the dominant elites of every tribe continue to define cultures in opposition to one other. After all, the hybrid threatens the stability of society and State, subverts the gospel truth of 'one people, one nation, one culture'.

Since the 19th century, the essentialist vision developed around the Hegelian '*Geist*' of a certain culture or nation, has haunted much of our thinking, and it continues to determine the political discourse. The hagiography of the nation-state, with its existential need for designated heroes and villains, and for self-definition through inner cohesion and outward enmity, [blanks out alternative and mutable narratives]. In the mausoleum of the nation-state, artists, philosophers and scientists are arrayed in a circle of timeless busts around the sarcophagus of national heritage. Outside, oblivious to and often in defiance of this official position, individuals and communities interact to form a living culture that is hybrid, innovative and confluential—as culture has always been.

Take the example of Greece and Turkey, two neighbours locked in conflict for centuries, sharing a history of ethnic cleansing. One of the worst cases of mass expulsion occurred in 1922. Hundred thousands of Greeks living in Turkey were forced to flee their homes in Smyrna, Istanbul and other cosmopolitan cities. They overflowed port-towns like Piraeus and Saloniki. Living in ghettos, these refugees carried in their bags an Oriental musical upbringing, which they adapted to suit a new home and a new audience. This music was to become the *Rembetiko*, the ultimate Greek *folk music*, a quaint and seemingly timeless tradition practised in the bars of the Aegean islands so favoured by Western tourists. But *rembetis* means 'underdog', and the songs dealt with pain, rebellion and loss, for many of the great singers and musicians—they met in hashish bars called *tekes*, the name for the dervish convents of the Sufis!—were social outcasts and drug addicts, who suffered imprisonment and exile under the dictatorship of Eleutherios Venizelos. Not least of all because of the satirical content of their songs, which criticised the military adventures of the dictator who lost his natural 'Asian' leg while trying to establish a foothold in Asia Minor, but who won, in this bizarre reversal of fortunes, the *Rembetiko*.

At the other end of Europe, Portugal's national musical form, the fado, developed from a mix of African, Brazilian and Iberian elements. Today's most famous fado singer, Mariza, argues that it is the product of a triangular route: a form carried by slaves from Africa to Brazil, where the Portuguese court was exiled during the Napoleonic wars and from there to Portugal with the court's return. Ironically enough, the fado was an integral feature of the Lusitanian culture brutally imposed on the African colonies by the dictator Salazar.

❧

In this book, we will demonstrate that confluence is the most vital and dynamic energy in the development of human culture. Confluence is to culture what gravity is to nature. Or in other words: No confluence, no culture. When culture is alive, it alters itself through inspirations from near and far, it changes course. Culture is the eternal shape-shifter. Only by interacting with the Other, can a culture keep itself alive. Thus, the greatest civilisations were built on confluence.

Take ancient Alexandria: Located at the pivot of many trade routes that connected Asia, Europe and Africa, Alexandria played host to Greek philosophers, Jewish commentators and Indian yogis. In this harbour-city, Ptolemy mapped the world and Eratosthenes measured its diameter, Euclid composed his treatise on geometry and a team of seventy-two Hellenised Jews produced the Septuagint, the first Greek translation of the Old Testament. The Septuagint was a memorable triumph, not only for Biblical scholarship, but also for Greek literature. In the Septuagint itself, we have shining examples of multi-ethnic and multi-religious civilisations such as Nebuchadnezzar's Babylon and Cyrus's Persia. During the Babylonian Captivity of the Jewish people, the prophet Daniel was raised by the god-king Nebuchadnezzar to the office of his high priest, exalted above all the local true-believing astrologer-priests (this is as if a mullah was anointed cardinal). In al-Andalus, during the 800-year period when Islam dominated most of Iberia, Muslims, Jews and Christians developed a sense of self by closely interacting with one another. Muslim rulers often employed Jews in important positions. One such was Samuel ha-Nagid, the 11th-century Grand Vizier of Granada, a rabbi, diplomat and soldier who led his largely Muslim troops into battle, yet also composed Hebrew secular poetry and Jewish liturgy. The second most important man, after the Emir, in this Islamic polity, he was at liberty to promote Jewish religious instruction and endow shrines in Jerusalem (this is as if the rabbi of the Synagogue in Berlin was appointed as minister of defence in Germany, and given Presidential permission to sponsor the education of young Jewish theologians in New York or Jerusalem). Despite its claim to unrivalled tolerance, the present-day West would find it very difficult to match the religious amplitude of Babylon or al-Andalus.

Repetition is the mother of dogma. Recently we have been fed the dogma of a long-standing Judaeo-Christian tradition. Despite the fact of frequent and harrowing textual and physical violence visited upon Jews by Christians in Europe for two millennia, despite the orthodox Jewish view of Christianity as a false chiliasm, and the triumphalist Christian belief that Judaism is a superseded religion because the Sanhedrin failed to recognise the true Messiah foretold by Isaiah. Serious theologians on both sides refute this secular invention as a 'contradiction in terms'. The portmanteau word 'Judaeo-Christian' was coined by US political pundits in the aftermath of World War II, on the far side of the Nazi death camps and the founding of Israel. Its inventors had a clear strategic eye on two objectives. First: to create an apparently inclusive and trans-denominational terminology that would overcome the accusation of anti-Semitism against a compromised US military-industrial Establishment, which had ignored the death camps despite credible evidence of their existence. And second: to bestow a respectable theological approval to a strategic alliance with Israel that would give the USA a firm grip on the jugular vein of the oil-rich Middle East while also providing a dependable front-line base against the Soviet bloc. Not surprisingly, given its origins in political expediency, the term 'Judaeo-Christian' is deceptively inclusive. It opens one door to the hybrid past of the Christian religion, but decisively shuts all the others. To depict accurately the rich textures of confluence that have been woven into the tapestry of Christianity, we would have to speak of an Egypto-Perso-Buddho-Judaeo-Islamo-Christian heritage.

In Chapter III (The Gifts of the Magi), we will travel back in time to the origins of the great monotheist religions, to the Babylonian Captivity of the Jewish people for example, to those 60 years of exile in Persia that profoundly changed the theology of Judaism. Almost all the elements of the Saviour narrative were invented by Zoroastrianism, the religion of ancient Persia. The Zoroastrian scriptures foretell the glorious coming of *Saoshyant*, the blessed one who will put an end to the march of sin. Saoshyant's mandate is to redeem the good from suffering and raise them to Heaven, to punish the evil with damnation in Hell, and so to inaugurate that magical future beyond time. When Cyrus the Great emancipated the Jewish people from their Babylonian Captivity, Saoshyant travelled west in their minds, to become the Messiah of Jewish thought and later, the Redeemer of the Christian faith.

The cosmic struggle between the armies of God and the armies of the Devil is, likewise, a centrepiece of Zoroastrian religious doctrine: Ahura Mazda, the wise God, does battle with Angra Mainyu, the evil one, until the end of time. Heaven and Hell were conceived first and very elaborately by ancient Persia's religious thinkers; the very word 'paradise' comes from the Persian '*peri-daeza*', the enclosed garden of the angels. The halo worn by the Risen Christ, and all the saints, was first used by Persian artists to distinguish divine and regal figures from mere mortals.

So when a Christian looks at an image of his Saviour, he sees a visual echo, an afterimage shaped by many images drawn from other religions and cultures that have gone before. He sees the result of a long process of confluence, the coming together of varied impulses. For what we perceive as the canonical and the classical is often a hybridity that we have forgotten. Or have been persuaded, encouraged, conditioned to forget.

We will also invoke the ancient Syrian god Adonis, sacrificed every spring to ensure a good harvest, whose temple was called the *Baith la-Haim* or House of Corn, a name that was enshrined in Christian lore as *Bethlehem*, the village where Jesus was born. His flesh and blood were distributed to the faithful, a symbolism incorporated into Christianity in the form of the Eucharist. We will open the ancestral cabinet of Christianity and find many forgotten names, such as that of Mithras: the solar deity who killed the bull of eclipse and was widely venerated by the legionaries of late-imperial Rome. His annual feast was celebrated on the date that came to be marked in the Gregorian calendar as 25 December. We will follow the fate of the *Buddha-charita* manuscript ('Life of the Buddha'), which travelled in the saddle-bags of merchants to the translation hub of Edessa in Asia Minor in the early centuries CE, from where the many miracles attributed to the Buddha came to be credited to Jesus Christ: walking on water, curing the diseased, calming the storm. The stories of the Buddha's previous lives, the Jatakas, also crossed the spine of the continent:

whenever you step into a museum or a Catholic church and
see St Hubert hypnotised by a stag bearing a cross, or St
Martin giving his richly embroidered cloak to a beggar, or
a tableau showing Barlaam and Josaphat, you are looking
at the Christian interpretation of themes first presented
in Buddhist literature in Afghanistan, Kashmir and North
India. And even the four Evangelical Gospels are profoundly
confluential as they were constructed from a mass of Essene,
Gnostic, Manichean, Apocryphal and proto-Christian
material floating around in the early centuries after Christ.

Examining India, we will travel with a Hindu of today back
in time to the perceived beginnings of his religion, only to find
that he is completely baffled by the strangeness of his Vedic
origins, which have nothing in common with his devotional
practice, iconography and worldview. Furthermore, we will
focus on the dynamic contributions of the Kushan Empire.
Lasting from the 1st to the 4th century CE, this little known
period sustained a remarkable confluential biosphere—a
compound of Graeco-Roman, Chinese, Persian and Indian
cultures—that dramatically changed the development of
Buddhist thought, practice and art, as well as Hindu doctrine
and iconography, besides acting as a clearing house for vital
interactions between Europe and East Asia.

VIOLENCE

However, we do not claim that confluence is necessarily a
peaceful process of embracing the Other and assimilating
heterogeneous impulses. We are certainly not imagining
a naïve pacifist ideal. Confluence is not without conflict;
rather, cultural transformation has been effected just as much
by peaceful encounter as by the tumults of war, invasion,

slavery, inquisition, pogrom and exile. Periods of deep confluence were not utopias of serenity and understanding among diverse groups brought together into a single polity. Take for example the musica negra of blues, jazz, rock, reggae and all that hip-hop. From the periphery of society, from the plantations and the ghettos, this music has come to dominate White American culture. Out of slavery and apartheid, the expressive music of the oppressed has become North America's greatest contribution to culture, and ironically a commodity, perfectly packaged and marketed by the transnational entertainment corporations.

Also, confluence does not imply complete understanding and coherent exchange. Marvellous cultural accomplishments have sprung from misconceptions and misunderstandings between individuals and societies. Actually, if one were to propagate a bill of basic rights for Culture, the right to misinterpretation would have to rank very high. Especially in the history of art, the artistic imagination has often been excited by forms from elsewhere excited, taking them out of their context and giving them new purpose. The West European painters and sculptors in the late 19th and early 20th centuries who discovered an ancient Egyptian *bas relief* sculpture, a Far Eastern print, or a West African figurine, were enthused by their expressive power, their stylisations of figure and space. They did not always have an understanding of the ritual or aesthetic significance of the artefacts. Nonetheless, they incorporated the aesthetic essence and revolutionised their own cultures. Thus the avant-garde experiments of Picasso, Braque and Kirchner were dynamised by West African and Oceanic sculpture; Matisse, Klee and Macke found a new language of motif and colour in North Africa and Turkey, and Kandinsky, Mondrian, Malevich were replenished by Asian spirituality, including yoga and Sufism. Modern European art is inconceivable without the deep immersion of its masters in the cultures from beyond the West.

In a previous generation, the radical young artists of Paris during the late 1880s, willing to rebel against the bourgeois salons of their time, embraced with profound curiosity a culture from the other side of the planet—a movement called *Japonisme*. Painters like Gauguin and Van Gogh admired the prints of Hokusai and Hiroshige. They internalised the compact, stylised figures, positioned asymmetrically in a shallow picture space, strong diagonals, and flat colouring with accentuated outlines. Japanese woodcuts, especially those depicting the *ukiyo-e* or 'floating world', the pleasure quarters of Tokyo and Kyoto, had become available with the opening up of trade between Japan and Europe. Interestingly, the Japanese prints had themselves been strongly influenced by Western techniques of perspective, foreshortening, Mannerist exaggeration, and the use of shading to suggest volume—techniques that filtered into Japan from West Europe via India and China. The great Hokusai (1760–1850), who studied these Western techniques carefully, was deeply interested in the mathematics of the visual, and kept himself *au courant* with the latest developments in European science; for instance, his colleague Ryutei Tanehiko notes in his diary of 1810 that he took lessons from Hokusai in the use of a Dutch mathematical instrument. When the works of Hokusai and Hiroshige found their way to Holland and France, they completed a loop and worked their way into the paintings of Monet, Manet, Van Gogh, Gauguin and Cezanne.

"CASUAL" CONNECTIVITY — KEY

Confluence does depend on a certain mobility of people, ideas, goods and services, as it relies on the presence of meeting places, junctions, nodes where everyday interaction with the Other is a fact of life, and you cannot ignore difference because you are surrounded by it, you live, eat and breathe it. It requires an interweaving of mercantile complicity, where each side needs the other to complete itself economically. A third precondition is an element of freedom from complacent dogma, and a basic curiosity and intellectual generosity: an interest, over and above the motives of gain and advantage, in that which is not the same, shared, or identically conditioned. In one word, we are describing an open system; the typical example of which is a harbour-city, none more famous than ancient Alexandria.

↳ NOT 100% SURE ABOUT CURIOSITY — ARE DIFFERENCES ALWAYS PERCEIVED?

But Alexandria fell to the knives of the bigots who assassinated its leading woman intellectual, Hypatia, and to the Christian zealots who burned down its great library: these men, although acting in the name of their religion, did not represent anything more sacred than the fear of the unfamiliar and rage at the threat posed to the citadels of their narrow belief by the pluralism of free thought. These men were tribalists, their insecurity and defensiveness matched only by their egotism and aggressiveness.

In Chapter III (The Ghetto of the Mind), we will analyse the powers of tribalism that have, throughout history, spelled the death of confluence. Everyone knows that Christopher Columbus sailed out to the 'New World' in 1492 CE, bankrolled by the joint powers of Castile and Aragon. This date was not fortuitous: in that same year, Castile and

Aragon had staged the so-called *Reconquista*, which had ended the 800-year marvel of al-Andalus and paved the way for the erasure of its richly hybrid culture. But the gifts of miscegenation were not so easily erased. As Columbus noted in his journal, the day he was assigned to command the voyage to the 'Indies' was the same day that the sovereigns of the New Spain ordered the expulsion of the Jews from their dominion. Thus, the Jews who had been encouraged by Muslim rulers to enact a religious and artistic renaissance were banished by Catholic rulers intolerant of difference.

Iberia never recovered from the cultural violence enacted in that year. The end of al-Andalus marked the establishment of a machinery of paranoia and persecution—the brutality of the Inquisition, the burgeoning of Spain's transcontinental empire, the barbaric slaughter of the Incas and the Aztecs, the plunder of the Orient and the Americas for gold, silver, spices and slaves were all to follow. Over time, every accomplishment that carried the fragrance of al-Andalus came to be regarded as mortal danger for Christendom. The Spanish Inquisition needed all the racks, thumbscrews and stakes at its disposal—for it was not simply fighting heretical tendencies within Christianity, but also extirpating the influence of Jews and Muslims. Its main task was to suppress the vigorous current of progressive thought that the Mediterranean confluence had set in motion. Only when Spain reclaimed its repressed confluential past, did it blossom again. Its greatest modern writer, Federico Garcia Lorca, saw himself as an heir to al-Andalus, he wrote *ghazals* and *qasidas*, two oriental poetic forms that were popular in the long-ago days, and the rhythm of his language mirrored the flamenco, a form of music and performance drawn from

Arab and Gypsy traditions that also inspired the greatest
Spanish composer, Manuel de Falla.

ॐ

Today, Alexandria is once again under threat from the bigots
and the zealots. The forces of tribalism once again menace
the open system so necessary for the flowering of confluence.
They resort to doctrines that narrow human potentiality to
a few clear options, all other choices being denigrated as
the work of the Devil. Among the weapons flourished by
this brand of tribalists, of whom the votaries of global jihad
are currently the most prominent, are an illiberal disdain
for dialogue, an intolerance of free expression, a negation
of women's rights, and a commitment to the erasure of all
religious and philosophical alternatives counterposed to their
own privileged reading of the true faith. The ideology of the
Christian Right and the exponents of the New American
Century is similar to the point of being identical with so-
called radical Islamism across the world and with Hindutva
in India. Through the first decade of the 21st century, the
Bush crusade and the Bin Laden jihad were equally colour-
blind to the world's polychrome diversity: these were twins in
terror, mirror images of the desire to narrow down, constrain
and strangle the cultural imagination. Such ideologies claim
to act in defence of a grand tradition, but they produce an
extremely narrow version of their religious and cultural
inheritance. They call for a return to fundamental truths
and original laws, but these are merely prescriptions and
proscriptions that they have invented by means of a selective,
even jaundiced, reading of the scriptures and testaments of
their traditions. Whether on the part of the Great Powers, or

the Guerrillas of Intolerance, the attitude towards cultural difference is the same: they will manipulate difference in order to regiment their own ranks, to divide their enemies, and to perpetuate conflicts that are profitable to an economy and soothing to a soul that revels in perpetual strife. Both kinds of tribalists claim the world as their playing ground and fight one another for control over it.

Also, we cannot uncritically support globalisation's claim of being all-inclusive, and to have achieved a fusion of heterogeneous cultural elements. This fusion is superficial, ersatz, false. Fusion is not confluence; it is a product of late capitalism, which has no interest in genuine diversity. The economic logic of globalisation calls for easy replication, for multiples based on a uniform pattern of variations, for universally executable programmes delivered with variable window dressing to make the locals everywhere feel at home with the new. The balance between global aspiration and local comfort is maintained through the gloss of glamour; and as the McDonald's model proves, nothing sells so well globally as the streamlined product presented in a streamlined manner.

It is a grave misconception to assume that globalisation has led to a deeper and more dynamic interaction between cultures. Capitalist globalisation has had a negative effect on pluralism: diversity is being diminished, languages and artistic expressions are dying out, alternative models of existence are only preserved in the dry tomes of academia.

❦

Today, with the crisscrossing of cultural impulses across the physical world and the Internet, every individual is a potential Alexandrian; an intercultural existence is the most productive form of existence. So that, when the custodians of national, civilisational or religious purity proclaim the end of the multicultural society, they are proclaiming the end of culture itself. The predicament of these custodians is most pathetic in Europe: for, by closing the gates of an open system, they are betraying the same great European traditions, advertised by Karl Popper in his influential writings, which they claim to represent.

The harbour-city is the archetypal image of confluence: it is the place where the river, the sum of numerous tributaries, meets the ocean. In our turbulent times, cosmopolitanism and cultural diversity are necessary conditions of existence— of being with others, of meeting the Other. Flowing with confluence, the individual realises gradually that the Other is not an enemy, not a stranger, not an alternative, and at times not even an Other, but just a mirror of the various possible faces, the multiple understandings of human existence, the varied definitions of belonging that can be arrived at. We must look into this mirror, not to lose ourselves in confusion, but to see ourselves and our options with greater clarity.

II

The Making of Europe

THE FORK AND OTHER MIXED BLESSINGS

Damned Easterners! Such snobs! So finicky pernickety.

Arrogant right down to the hem of their stolas. Who did this hussy think she was? Just because Domenico Selvo, groomed to be the future Doge, had chosen her as his bride. Granted, the court circles of Constantinople, where her father was a high official, were rather sophisticated. But did that mean that she could defy natural courtesy and insist on her ridiculous fashions? She actually had the nerve to refuse to eat with her fingers at the wedding feast. Instead, she had ordered her fawning eunuch—another perversion, in God's name, what next?—to cut her food into morsels, so that she could spear each morsel with that piddling golden doodah she held between her fingers, carry it to her mouth, lips touched metal ... no more, it was disgusting beyond belief. Everybody in the grand chamber was scandalised. No one more so than cardinal bishop Peter Damian, a man of God if there ever was one, who lost no time in warning his flock against this abomination: 'God in his wisdom has provided man with natural forks—his fingers. Therefore it is an insult to Him to substitute artificial metallic forks for them when dining.' Besides, as he pointed out, it was useless for eating spaghetti. No wonder that this Byzantine princess, Maria Argyropoulina by name, died before very long of some wasting disease. The future saint, Peter Damian, sermonised grimly over 'the Venetian Doge's wife, whose body, after her excessive delicacy, entirely rotted away'. Vanitas vanitatum!

Verily, the fork and the West did not hit it off well. After this early censure from the pulpit of the Church, the fork vanished into the kitchen cabinet, not to emerge again until three centuries later. When necessary, food was cut and speared with the knife. It was not until the 16th century that the fork asserted its culinary presence in Italy. By then, the upper class of Italy had developed a new preoccupation with hygiene; it was proper for a guest to bring his own fork and spoon to the banquet, elegantly kept in a box called the *cadena*. The rest of Christian Europe was oblivious to the blessing of this utensil, until Catherine de' Medici married—weddings seem to be focal points of cultural dissemination—Henry I of France in 1533. Her dowry included silver dinner forks wrought by Benvenuto Cellini, the famed Italian goldsmith. The French court continued to distrust this dangerous innovation, right up to the time of King Louis XIV, who relied on his fingers and a knife.

In the East the fork had passed into polite usage at some point in the 4th century in Byzantium, and was common amongst the affluent of West Asia from the 7th century onwards. Even the Tartars were versed in the art of the fork, as a letter by a Franciscan monk to Louis IX of France testifies. Today, the fork marks a cultural boundary, and people who continue to use their fingers are marvelled at, as at best charmingly quaint. As if to vindicate the long-ago bishop's warning, a recent study has established that the fingers exude a certain enzyme that helps digestion. But of course, we would not even dream of forsaking this utensil, which is not only essential to our eating habits, but also an integral part of our lifeworld. There are many cultural imports like the fork—toothpaste and sugar, the coffeehouse and the garden, carpets and perfumes, fountains and libraries—which were brought into the West from elsewhere but are now held to be unquestionably 'European'. Although objects are not adapted to the same degree as ideas, stories, songs or images, they are domiciled and naturalised in a similar way. First, they are met with suspicion and treated as mixed blessings. Then follows a wary provisional acceptance. And finally, there is a rapturous embrace of what was once foreign, to the point that its alien origin is forgotten. This is a necessary and healthy process. Were it not for the fact that the tines of the fork are used to jab at the Other. Often, the potted histories purposely erase the foreign influence. To remember where something came from is to acknowledge the many sources of culture and the many debts that each civilisation owes others. And the vivid awareness of our formative hybridity reminds us that we will always need cultural provocation and enrichment from foreign sources. The fork certainly does not symbolise a parting of ways, but a continuous anticipation of the new.

The Womb of the East

The Idea of Europe

The general assumption of most Europeans is that Europe is the centre of the world. The history of the last five centuries seems to bear them out. Without Europe there would have been no Renaissance, no Enlightenment, no French Revolution, no Industrial Revolution and no upsurge of Modernity. In many respects, the imperial realities support this perception. The European powers have conquered the greater part of the globe, their languages have been transplanted into foreign soils and their systems of education and administration have been installed everywhere, including the USA, much as it might proclaim a unique destiny today. And even nations that rebuffed imperialism like China are not immune to the influences of Europe. After all, the People's Republic of China was long governed according to the ideas of a lawyer's son from Trier. To be international is in great measure to be European—or, the other way around: what is European is universal. The rest is dismissed as regional.

Although Christianity is 2,000 years old, the concept and reality of a Christian Europe is less than half that age. The transformation of 'Mediterranea' into the continent of 'Europa' forms one of the most intriguing chapters in the history of political assertion and cultural identity. From the beginning of civilisational time, the Mediterranean, which is as much of an ocean as Europe is a continent, was defined by a system of interrelationships that linked its littoral regions: Crete formed a symbiosis with Pharaonic Egypt, Phoenicians ploughed the sea of mercantile profitability, Hellenic cities used the mines of Iberia, Romans and Carthaginians maintained an alternate trade-and-hate relationship. Being used to regarding reality through maps, we tend to see the blue stretch of water as a division; more often, it is a fluid bridge. Throughout this book, we will cite instances of the tremendous cultural traffic that crossed this bridge in either direction.

The current reductionism, which narrows the complex diversity of Islam down to relatively recent and reactionary tendencies like Wahabbism, should not obscure the fact that, for centuries, Islam was the most progressive cultural force in the Mediterranean region and West Asia. Its achievements were not necessarily Arab in origin—as we will show, Persian, Indian and Greek influences abound—but they were all Islamic by translation, incubation and diffusion. The difference between the Islamic and the Christian world was often that between openness and closure, urban sophistication and rural gaucherie, mobility and inertia, between a predominantly mercantile and a largely feudal economy. The permeable boundary between the Mediterranean world and the cultural wasteland to its north ran somewhere along the line where the olive tree ceases to grow. The Anglo-Saxons, the Franks, the Teutons and the Vikings were the main factors of this 'developing world' in the northern hemisphere. The Normans played out an alternate historical destiny: they were candidates for the emerging market of those days, and linked the two worlds. Thus, the shift of gravity from Mediterranea to Europa also marks the change from a sea-based economy of exchange to the notion of a bulwark or fortress land-mass, to be secured against invaders.

Having achieved so much, it is understandable that Europe should believe it has achieved it all on its own. Furthermore, because of the notable successes of the French and British colonial empires and the spread of knowledge systems perfected in centres like Paris, Berlin, Vienna, London and

Rome, we are led to believe that Europe has always been powered by its central and western parts.

It must be reiterated that the Mediterranean region is not the seam of Europe, to be double- and treble-folded and sewn firmly against the rest of the world—but rather, a creative and productive intermediate zone of crossings, where networks of relationships flowered and fresh creations came to birth. The foundations of European culture would not have been possible without the permeable, mutable and sometimes even symbiotic qualities of its borders. All the same, we have come to regard fluid forms, unstable identities and blurred definitions as a problem. The public discourse on Europe inclines increasingly towards a demand for clear categories of membership, coherent clarifications regarding the distinguishing marks of belonging. It also allows for the rise of a border-checkpoint mentality, to differentiate European from non-European. In preparing for the future, we ought to grasp that borders are confluences that we have fertilised in the past; that they are playing fields of hybrid cultures, which have performed a defining role in the development of continents. Because what we regard as alien, at any time, is always only the result of a momentary difference, a fleeting gesture of history.

What is this Europe, which we speak of every day, without having a clear picture of it? Europe is the only peninsula in the world that has leaped to the status of a continent. It is named after Europa, a Phoenician princess, the daughter of King Agenor, an offspring of Poseidon who renounced Egypt, crossed the sea and settled in the land of Canaan. Amazing as the myth of Europe is, the princess has not become famous for an exercise of her own will, but rather, for the fate that overtook her when she was abducted by Zeus. The legend of Europa has known many versions. The scenes and threads of action may change, its characters tread softly through the chronicles of Apollodorus, are sung of by Pindar and creep through folklore; the moral and political tenor of the material varies. Because Europe has been like this from the very beginning: a diversity; and its history can become sacred to all, only when it can be told in such a way that it carries a special meaning for everyone.

Alpu Betu Gamu

Long, long ago, the Mother of Wisdom found herself alone and melancholy. Her name was Sophia. Unhappy with the state of the world, she arose and created from within herself a parallel world of unprecedented splendour. Such, in a nutshell, is the traditional account of Ancient Greece's origin and uniqueness. This elevated civilisation, the account continues, became the soul of Europe and the source of its global supremacy. But classical Greece could hardly have had an immaculate conception. For centuries, the rhapsodising of European intellectuals over Greece went hand in hand with complete lack of interest in where it was rooted and where its inspirations had come from. Greece was pure white! Even the temples were whitewashed, so that they could shine forth from their cliffs. In truth, they were richly painted in the period of their apogee, and resembled nothing more closely than the highly ornate facades of Hindu temples in South India. It is now known that the keepers at the British Museum, during the 19th century, 'improved' their Greek marbles by scrubbing them with carborundum to eliminate all traces of paint. A pronounced measure of racism biased imperial scholarship: Mesopotamia was a respectable origin for Judaic culture, but how could Aryan Greece have been inspired by Semitic culture? Or even African culture, since some scholars had been whispering about the links between Egypt and Greece? Once Classicism became an ersatz religion, it was only consistent that the genius of Hellas assumed god-like omnipotence.

In recent years there has been a tectonic shift in perception. Scholars from many disciplines have challenged the de-contextualised worship of the Antique. The archaeologists ploughing the fields of rural Turkey during the last few decades have dug up truckloads of proof that there were far more polises in Asia Minor than previously assumed, and that their contribution to the development of Greek civilisations was not incidental but essential. Hellas consisted in the initial phase of a multitude of city-states and small kingdoms; but of the 1,500 Greek cities, only 200 were in the Aegean, while the other 1,300 were scattered around the rest of the Mediterranean and the Black Sea. Although Athens and Sparta stood on the European side of the Aegean, Greece became Hellas because of cities like Ephesus, Miletus, Rhodos, Halikarnasos and Ilion, which were situated along the coastline of today's Turkey. The cities of Asia Minor were not only far more affluent than those of the Greek mainland, but they were able to interact closely with the myriad cultures and traditions of Western Asia, above all the Persian. Out of this prolonged exchange the Hellenistic civilisation was created. The recent archaeological research underlines what some authors have always asserted on the basis of common sense. Homer 'as a finished achievement was a product of Ionia', a region in today's Western Turkey,

'... the most important part of the Hellenic world', Bertrand Russell writes (Russell 1966, 33, 48). Thales, with whom philosophy is usually said to have begun, was a citizen of Miletus, then a bustling cosmopolis of 60,000 inhabitants with four different harbours. He won fame by predicting an eclipse, a feat of genius one would deem, were it not for the close relations between Miletus and Babylon (through Lydia), where astronomers had already ascertained that eclipses follow a cycle of about 19 years. Thales was the founding father of the first philosophical school of Hellas, the famous Milesian school, which flourished until the beginning of the 5th century BCE, when Persia conquered the region. Other centres like Colophon, Pergamon, Magnesia and Philadelphia were situated in the heart of Asia Minor. And the town Europos was a trade-polis on the banks of the Euphrates, in today's Iraq—this invests 'Europe' with the symbolic charge of an important intersection and transit point along the great avenues of human passage, and not a self-satisfied fortress at the land's end of Asia.

Conservative authors have tended to gloss over the 'inconvenient location' of these flourishing centres by labelling them as 'outposts on the borders' of the Hellenistic culture, implicitly claiming the status of a 'centre' for Athens long before it became the powerhouse of Hellenistic civilisation. Many of the events in Greek mythology, in as far as they are geographically fixed, take place at these supposed fringes, and even beyond. Medea for example puts the dragon to sleep in Colchis, near Mt Elbrus, the highest peak of the Caucasus. Croesus, the 'richest man in the world', is king of Lydia, today on Turkey's west coast. The legend notes that he was treated fairly by his generous enemy, Cyrus the Persian, but fails to explain how he made his extraordinary fortune. Midas, who craves to have everything he touches turn into gold, is king of Phrygia, in today's west-central Anatolia. The setting of its myths offers clues to the prehistory of a people.

The dogmatic scholars pointed a sharp spotlight on Ancient Greece, as the single heroic actor declaiming a monologue, radiant on a stage otherwise plunged in impenetrable darkness. Now that the stage is bathed in a more diffuse light, we see all the other actors in the drama: Mesopotamians, Persians, Egyptians and Phoenicians. We understand that Ancient Greece was engaged in numerous dialogues as part of a polyphonic script. The vastly enhanced state of knowledge has enabled linguists, mythologists and classical historians to name the oriental heritage of Ancient Greece as such, to demonstrate the intimate connections of Greece with the trading and manufacturing networks of West Asia and the Eastern Mediterranean. The golden fleece, Midas' affliction, Croesus' treasures, the rain of gold in Danae's bedchamber— all descend from the empyrean of myth into the reality of commercial exchange. Suddenly, the streams of influence are evident: 'What was until recently a marginal subject has, in the last few years, become the subject of diverse and very vigorous international scholarship' (Burkert 2003, 5).

Earlier on, many Greek words pertaining, for example, to weights, measures and nautical technology were said to be of uncertain origin; now a competent comparison reveals that these are perfectly intelligible as Semitic loans. Recently, scholars like Walter Burkert have pointed out the abundant similarities: Greek ideas have roots in Sumerian and Akkadian mythology. The epic of *Gilgamesh* and the

Homeric texts share formulaic verses, epithets, soliloquies of the heroes, and invocations. The seven giants who rise up against the high god Marduk reappear as the seven titans (the word itself derived from the Akkadian *titu*) who rebel against Zeus. Other myths found in their earliest form in Mesopotamia and later in Greece include the story of a goddess falling in love with a mortal, and that of a hero entering a sacred grove to fight its guardian for the treasure deposited there.

Few cultural achievements can match the invention of the alphabet in importance. While it is impossible to date the invention of the modern alphabet precisely, we do know for certain that Semitic-speakers in the Levant had arrived, by the 11th century BCE, at the idea that language can be comprehensively represented by 25 phonetic signs. The first such alphabet was used for the Phoenician-Canaanite, Hebrew and Aramaic languages, and its use expanded in the 10th century BCE. Its inventors came up with the inspired idea of linking each phoneme with a memorable association from everyday life. The sound for 'a' was associated with *alpu*, meaning 'ox', 'b' with *betu*, meaning 'house', 'g' with *gamu*, meaning 'camel'. The Phoenicians had already established a web of trading posts in the East Mediterranean, and to do business in this increasingly complex world, the Greeks realised they would need to rely on more than the individual memory that had served earlier, the mnemonic archives that generations of traders had carried in their minds and on their tongues. The heroic world was yielding before a more pragmatic world: contracts, bills of lading and lists of goods were growing longer and their terms more complicated. The Greeks would have to write things down, if they were going to keep up with the competition. And so, shortly after 800 BCE, they decided to adapt to change and begin writing in the 'Phoenician style'. Curiously though, they chose to replicate the symbols of each letter—although *alpha*, *beta*, *gamma* had no meaning in their language, the names and forms of the characters remained more or less identical. Within a few decades of the introduction of the Greek alphabet, the new skill had spread across the whole Greek-speaking Mediterranean world. The Phrygians, Lydians and Lycians to the east borrowed it, as did the Etruscans and Iberians to the west. 'In principle,' Burkert writes, 'the old comic strip of "ox" and "house", invented by some Semite in the Bronze Age, has remained in place until today. Even our computers respect it.' (Burkert 2003, 27)

In mythology, this development is linked to the story of Europa. Her father Agenor despatched his son Cadmus to search for her, instructing him not to return until he had found his abducted sister. But Zeus had concealed his captive only too well, and Cadmus, fed up with his futile search, settled down in Greece, where he founded the city of Thebes. Legend says that he carried the alphabet with him into exile: a metaphor for the Asian cultural influence on Greece, which was for a long time regarded as merely fabular. But recent finds in Thebes have confirmed the historical core of the myth.

Ancient Greece not only sprang from diverse origins, but it also spread very far. Barely had Greek civilisation established itself, when it wove a net across the whole Mediterranean. And after Alexander the Great came to power, this net was extended across most of the then known world, over deltaic Egypt and across the plains and highlands of West Asia, all the way to north-western India. To describe the knots of this net as Greek colonies is to misunderstand them completely. The Greek settlements in Asia and North Africa were not dependent, either for material sustenance or ideological coherence, on a single point of origin. They redefined the relationship of the periphery to the centre: Delphi and Salamis, Macedonia and the Peloponessus were only points of departure for many Greeks after Alexander; the real centres were almost all to be found on the periphery. The soldiers, merchants and scholars who had gone out into this expanding empire may have begun life as Greeks, but most of them lost no time in redefining themselves by hyphenation with the magnificent cultures in which they found themselves—Egypt, Persia and India. The sphere of influence had become a web of confluence. Remapped in the light of this realisation, Ancient Greece is seen, not as the singular source of European civilisation, but as one among a series of cultural forces that changed artistic, religious, philosophical and political expression from the Bay of Biscay to the Bay of Bengal. The fork of historical evolution took Greece to the East and, later, Islam, charged with a Perso-Indo-Greek momentum, to the West. If one were determined to reduce the complex DNA of cultures to one strand, one could just as easily claim that Islam is the basis of the West and Greece is the basis of the East. But this of course would be as absurd as the conventional wisdom. Between one blindness and the other lies the reality of confluence.

൸

Cities like Edessa in Asia Minor and Alexandria in the Nile Delta best convey the strength and depth of these currents of confluence. Edessa was the name that the Seleucids, Alexander's successors in the region, gave this city; today's Sanhurfa, an important trading centre on the Silk Route, claimed by some to be the birthplace of Abraham. In the early centuries of the Current Era, it became a great university town, whose scholars came from Persia, India and Central Asia, contributing to a cross-fertilisation of ideas. 'There was a marked influence of Persian and Indian ideas on Edessa's theology, and its theological school became notorious for the dangerous heterodoxy of its teachings. In this cosmopolitan environment, the city's most notorious heretic, Bardaisan of Edessa, was able to write an accurate account of the dietary regimes of Hindu priests and Buddhist monks, while Indian stories and legends came to be written down in unexpected new Christian incarnations' (Dalrymple 2000, 66). We do not know when it happened, but the day the first copy of *The Life of the Buddha* found its way to the University of Edessa, in the saddle-bags of caravan merchants and itinerant monks, was certainly a bright day. This biography written by a monk called Asvaghosha (see the sub-chapter 'A Body for the Buddha') in what is today Afghanistan, was translated by some of the eclectic scholars of Edessa and from here passed into Christian as well as Islamic tradition, as we will see.

Alexandria too, in the early centuries of the Current Era, was a festival of competing cults and merging beliefs. The catacombs of Kom el Shogafa bear witness to this amazing religious remix: the Greek sarcophagus is guarded by Egyptian gods wearing Roman armour. 'Situated at the meeting place of trade routes linking both Asia and Africa with Europe it was quite natural that the city should be a centre of intellectual ferment. Indian sadhus wandered its streets, debating with Greek philosophers, Jewish exegetes and Roman architects. It was here that Euclid wrote his treatise on geometry, that Eratosthenes measured the diameter of the world (he was only fifty-four miles out), that Ptolemy produced his astonishing maps and that a great team of seventy-two Hellenistic Jews produced the Septuagint, the first Greek translation of the Old Testament.' (Ibid., 385).

Cast into this teeming bazaar of ideas, the philosophy of Plato had to come down from the elevated reaches of the Athenian Academy into the buzz of the agora. Plato had to take his chances among those who championed Upanishadic monism, Buddhist ethics, Zoroastrian eschatology, and Christian salvationism. The Romanised Jews were striving for a way to combine the ancient faith with a new cultural coating. The early Christians were still shaping their faith, open in all directions, gradually acquiring a taste for philosophical sophistication when answering those trained in the Greek schools. Out of this churning emerged the Jewish Platonist thinker—contemporary both of Jesus Christ and of St Paul—Philo Judaeus or Philo of Alexandria (c. 25 BCE–c. 50 CE), whose chief contribution was to synthesise Platonic, Stoic and Judaic ideas (see the sub-chapter 'The Eternal Construction Site'). This vision would serve as a foundation, not only for Christian, but also for later Jewish and Muslim rational theologians.

On the Alexandrian intellectual bourse, prices for all ideas fluctuated under pressure from a saturated and diversified market. Plato's stock stood high, but there was an urgent need to repackage him for the changing times. This was the mandate that Plotinus (c. 205–270 CE), a Hellenised Egyptian who had studied in Alexandria, took up. Plotinus spared neither expense nor effort, travelling all the way to Iran to study the doctrines of the Persians and the Indians. His disciple Porphyry has acknowledged these influences. Plotinus' ideas on the soul, especially his doctrine of '*duo sunt in homine*' ('there are Two within man', the conception that every self comprises a higher nature partaking of the purity of Form, and a lower nature partaking of the corruptibility of matter) were not only derived from Plato, but also reflected the teachings of the Upanishads.

Plotinus compares the Transcendent to the sun and the soul to the moon, their relationship much the same as that between *Brahman*, the eternal Overself, and *atman*, that fraction of the Overself that is manifested within the individual. The sun sends out its rays and thus changes everything, but remains unaffected by what it creates. Like the Indian mystics, he believed that the soul can only unite itself with the Transcendent through ecstasy (*henosis*), and not through thought. Plotinus' ideal man, the 'Proficient', who embodies equanimity and never sways between happiness and sorrow, has much in common with the Bhagavad Gita's ideal of the 'one wisely unmoved by circumstance', indifferent equally to elation and grief. (This in turn inspired Rudyard Kipling to write the words famously engraved above the entrance to the centre court at Wimbledon: 'If you can meet with Triumph and Disaster/ And treat those two impostors just the same'). Plotinus' teaching that happiness consists in a 'flight from this world's ways and things' and that the soul must 'disengage itself from the body and disdain its nominal goods' (*Enneads* I.4.14) constitutes a dramatic departure from the Hellenic adoration of the *physis*. It can only be explained as a strong affinity with the extreme asceticism of the Jainas, who were doubtless among the *gymnosophistai*, the naked wise men from India, settled in Alexandria at that time. For in this Indian religion, the hermits called the *digambara* are draped in nothing but the sky.

In the centuries to come, the ideas of Plotinus and of Philo would travel with greater vigour eastward, to Baghdad and elsewhere, since there were no takers in the West at that time. The previously receptive Christian mind was closing fast. The great library and museum complex of Alexandria, founded in the 3rd century BCE by the Ptolemid dynasty in Egypt, was burned down during a civil war in the late 3rd century CE, and what survived of it, a daughter library, was burned down by rampaging Christian fundamentalists in 391 CE. To be sure, the Byzantine emperor, Julian the Apostate, had been an enthusiastic Platonist and re-established Plato's Academy in Athens at the end of the 4th century CE—but this was a shortlived phenomenon. Like the Apostate's own career, it too came to an end at the hands of Christian religious fanaticism.

The fanaticism on the street reflected a clash of ideas on a higher level. While Greek philosophy had concerned itself with observation and deduction, with doubt and scepticism, with experiment and hazard, the established dogma of Christianity undertook the exact opposite. Reality needed to be pressed into the fold of revelation. Truth was not something to wrestle with, but an ordinance to be dutifully applied. Thus instruments of the Ancients were obsolete, or even dangerous.

And no dissent would be tolerated, once the imperial

Confluences

centre had enshrined its vision of truth as dogma. This was the lesson of 489 CE, when the Byzantine emperor Zeno destroyed the University of Edessa. This home of intercultural discourse—where Bardaisan the heretic had used Babylonian, Persian, Platonic and Christian components to build a motor of free will that could circumvent fate and nature—became a casualty of the fratricidal conflict among Christ's interpreters. Zeno was a Trinitarian, the scholars of Edessa were Nestorian: they had refused to bend their beliefs to his will, and paid the price. Taking what manuscripts they could, and carrying the rest in their heads, the Edessa scholars found refuge in the Sassanian Empire, settling eventually into the university of Gondeshapur (founded 271 CE, in today's Khuzestan, south-west Iran), which enjoyed the distinction of having the world's earliest known teaching hospital, as well as renowned faculties of medicine, astronomy and mathematics. The Nestorians taught and researched here for generations to come—Sassanian Iran fell, Abbasid Baghdad became the crest-jewel of the world—and they joined in a translation project by which knowledge acquired from Platonic Athens and polyglot Alexandria, meticulously refined in Edessa and Gondeshapur, fed into Baghdad, and later travelled all the way to Cordoba, Palermo, Venice, thus into the heart of Christian Europe and into modernity.

Classical philosophy came to an end with two cataclysmic events: in 524 CE, Theodoric, the Ostrogoth overlord of Italy, ordered the execution of his chief civil servant, Boethius, who was the last Platonic philosopher of note of the Antique. Shortly afterwards, in 529 CE, the Byzantine Emperor Justinian ordered the closure of the schools of 'pagan philosophy' in Athens, expelling their scholars from the city.

The last lamps of classical philosophy were extinguished. The only repositories of Greek learning now were outside Christendom: Gondeshapur in Sassanian Iran and Buddhist Nalanda in India; not counting a small, menaced outpost in Ireland, at Europe's westernmost fringe.

A Thousand and One Thoughts

[handwritten margin note: So strange to antique / reductionist history / and simultaneously do it]

By the 7th century CE, Europe had spiralled into an abyss of stagnation. The western portion of the continent was in thrall to successive waves of barbarian invaders, some of them nominally Christianised but many holding on to their tribal beliefs, all taking the imperial symbol of old Rome as their target: Vandals, Visigoths, Alans, Huns. On the other side of Christian Europe, the Eastern Roman Empire was locked in a prolonged war of attrition with the Sassanian Empire, which fatigued both combatants. The Church was in intellectual stasis, permitting only narrow readings of Holy Writ. The monks were hiding in their retreats, turned inward. The mental atmosphere was one of embattlement and threat. All erudition and secular education had been lost: there was no science to speak of, and certainly no curiosity, only a dread concerning the new and the strange.

How then did this intellectual graveyard become the seedbed for one of the most extravagantly dynamic accomplishments of human culture, which began about four centuries later? How could this desert have come to flower without rain? The answer, surprising and even shocking as this might sound today, is that there was rain, in the form of Islam. With their boundless energy and firmness of belief, the early warriors of Islam reanimated the reservoirs of the Sassanian and the Roman Empires. Synergies flourished in new situations, as the desert-dwelling conquerors recognised the need to rely on existing expertise to govern their newfound dominions. Thus the Arabs unleashed pragmatic and cultural energies that had been lying in somnolence, offering bureaucrats, poets, architects, philosophers and translators renewed professional challenges as well as fresh horizons to strive towards. Less than a century after its founding in 622 CE, Islam had shaken up the world from Iberia to India, including much of Euro-Asian culture in a sky-wide tent. Within the first few centuries of its existence, Islam, in conjuncture with existing traditions, would give the world marvels that take the breath away: scientific advances, philosophical speculations, grand mosques, exquisite palaces, irrigation systems and manuals of astronomy, the beginnings of robotics and the refinement of surgery, and several distinctive dynastic and regional styles, the Umayyad, the Abbasid and the Fatimid among them.

Abbasid Baghdad (762–1258 CE) became the seat of the Caliphate and therefore the centre of the Islamic *umma*. It was the capital of the leading civilisation of its time, and the world's most important translation centre. The wealth of Abbasid culture was certainly due to many factors, but the most important seems to have been location. Baghdad was nourished by a series of past confluences, as well as by a net of trade and communication. Ships from all over the known world, from China, India, Russia, Malaya, Africa, Byzantium and from the entire Islamic empire docked at Basra on the Persian Gulf, not far from where the Tigris and the Euphrates meet, delivering as much as they carried away. The first Arabic universities were established here, and schools of poetry flourished. 'Briefly, the wealth, the diversity of races, the amalgam of cultures and the new ideas which flooded into Baghdad during this period led to an assault on established value, the encouragement of hedonism and innovation in art (Wightman & al-Udhari 1976, 19).

The influential Barmecide family incarnates the cultural dynamics of Abbasid Baghdad. The Barmecides, recent converts from the Persian branch of Buddhism called the Naubahar ('new garden', from the Sanskrit *nava-vihara*), had supported the Abbasid cause from the beginning. They became viziers to Caliph al-Mahdi and his successor Harun al-Rashid. The family name is an Arabisation of the Sanskrit *paramaka*, abbot. They had been the hereditary custodians of the revered Naubahar monastery in Balkh (today in north Afghanistan). By adapting the Buddhist institution of the *vihara* ('garden', a dwelling-place and school for monks), they introduced the *medersa*, which became the educational base of Islam. And by supporting scientists from Gondeshapur and extolling the example of the Northern Indian university library of Nalanda—they revived the Sassanian custom of inviting Indian scholars to share their learning—the Barmecides not only promoted the growth of one of humankind's legendary libraries, but also set in motion the massive translation project that accompanied it. Their proximity to the throne, the prestige they enjoyed because of their wealth, generosity and public service, and the lingering suspicion that they were pseudo-Muslims who had never renounced their Buddhist past, all conspired against the Barmecides. Within the span of three decades (775–803 CE), this vizierial dynasty was raised to the heights of power, stung by the 'scorpions of envy', and felled by conspiracy and assassination. They left traces of their grandeur in that perennial Baghdad classic, the *Thousand and One Nights*, in the connoisseur of illusions who dominates 'The Barmecide's Feast', and in Jafar, Harun al-Rashid's vizier. But the lasting contribution of the Barmecides was the cultural transformation they had launched: it was a masterful djinn and no zealous guardian of faith was strong enough to push it back into its lamp.

The spirit of the Barmecides was continued by al-Mamun, Harun's successor on the Caliphal throne, who founded a new academy on the banks of the Tigris in 832 CE: the *Bait ul-Hikma*, the 'House of Wisdom'. Here, massive numbers of manuscripts from every conceivable field of learning were translated from Sanskrit, Greek, Syriac and Persian into Arabic: collections of fables, repertories of herbs and drugs, anthologies of poetry, philosophical investigations, astrological speculations, alchemical digests, astronomical tables. Gondeshapur graduates staffed the translation enterprise, among the best known being Hunayn ibn Ishaq (d. 873 CE), an Arab Nestorian from what is today Southern Iraq. Called Johannitius by his future Latin editors in Toledo, Hunayn translated numerous Greek medical works, including the testaments of Galen, and many of these are now known only through him. Surrounded by such a comprehensive collection of human knowledge, the intellectuals of the Islamic world expanded eagerly on it.

Perhaps in no other field was their contribution of greater consequence than in philosophy. Traditionally, the influence of the Arab philosophers of the 9th to the 12th centuries is regarded as one of trusteeship, as if they were merely looking after the Aristotelian cat while the West was on an extended holiday. In reality, original philosophical thought in the

West died with the execution of Boethius and the closure
of the schools of Athens, and was resurrected triumphantly
in Baghdad, and further refined in Cordoba, Granada
and Toledo. The rehearsals for the Renaissance began in
Baghdad, inaugurated by a school of Arab philosophers who
had been influenced by Aristotle, and who called themselves
the *falasifa* (singular: *faylasuf*). These were courageous men
who defied the claims of faith and upheld those of reason,
who insisted on the primacy of individual inquiry and
discrimination, not hesitating to question or even mock the
proclaimed supremacy of revelation. Many of them were not
ethnic Arabs, but of Persian, Tajik or Turkmen origin, but all
were born Muslim and wrote primarily in Arabic, regarding
themselves as members of the ecumene of Islam. Polymaths
with universal interests, they were beneficiaries of, and
contributors to, the garnering of intellectual resources that
was being accomplished in Baghdad.

At the very fountainhead of Islamic philosophy stands
al-Kindi (801–866 CE). A Baghdadi aristocrat and the first
faylasuf, he interested himself in medicine, astrology and
Indian mathematics; most importantly, he drew a creative
and empowering conclusion from the philosophical work
of the Alexandrian Neoplatonists. To the rational mind
working in a system dominated by faith, the arguments of
Plotinus could be used as follows: all issues pertaining to
the One (or God, or Perfection) can be entrusted to those
best qualified to deal with it, namely the theologians and
the mystics. The man of reason assures them that, since the
material world is less than perfect, it does not deserve their
attention, and is best left to others. Thus, while apparently
accepting the limitations of reason and honouring the

theologians and mystics, the philosopher at one stroke also confines them to their specialisation and opens the vast field of human experience for himself—he is free to establish criteria for the uncovering and usefulness of knowledge, to discuss perceptions of goodness, beauty, happiness, balance, mutuality and justice. This turn towards the material and empirical also meant that many of the *falasifa* turned naturally to Plato's disciple Aristotle, whose rational and scientific bent of mind they found more congenial than his guru's fondness for abstraction.

Al-Kindi declared: 'We should not be ashamed to acknowledge truth from whatever source it comes to us, even if it is brought to us by former generations and foreign peoples. For him who seeks the truth there is nothing of higher value than truth itself.' As the historian Albert Hourani notes, this view expresses an intellectual excitement, a heightened receptivity as well as the self-assurance of a culture that was secure in its imperial power and in its belief in divine guidance (Hourani 2002, 76–77).

Al-Kindi's successor, Rhazes (al-Razi, 865–923 CE), was even more radical, claiming that 'human reason alone can give certain knowledge, the path of philosophy is open to all uses, the claims of revelation are false, and religions are dangerous.' Rhazes was the chief physician to the Caliph in Baghdad, an enthusiast of Epicurus, a healer who founded his medical theories in empirical observation and experiment. He argued that claimants to special revelation were prone to intolerance and violence in its defence, while reason, being potentially available to all, was God's best provision of judgement and self-restraint. Similarly, his contemporary Alfarabius (al-Farabi, 878–c.950) was convinced that philosophy had no future anywhere in the world except within the dynamic milieu of Islamic thought, where it could gain a new lease of life. Although he accepted the validity of both the Koran and the thought of Plato and Aristotle (he is venerated in the Muslim World as the 'Second Teacher' after Aristotle), he taught that Islam, as religion, was not by itself sufficient for a philosopher's needs. In his view, religion brought truth to ordinary people in symbolic form, for the truth in its pure form is not accessible to their limited intellects. But to the philosopher, human reason is necessarily superior to theology. No one would have voiced such reasoning in Europe at that time.

These thinkers prepared the path for Avicenna (Ibn Sina, 980–1037 CE), among the greatest minds of the era we call the Middle Ages. The materials that Avicenna had at his disposal were Plato, Aristotle, the Neoplatonist Plotinus and the Koran. His crisis was that of reconciling reason with revelation, in the context of an Islam whose high ground was already being claimed by two rival monopolies: the politically ambitious jurist-theologian on the one hand, and the God-intoxicated mystic on the other. Avicenna's fundamental problem was: How to balance philosophy's restless mobility with faith's absolute sense of anchorage? This physician and philosopher produced an Aristotelian defence of speculative inquiry. In the context of religious law, he and his successor Averroes argued that the process of interpretation, demonstration and application of principles—and the building up of a body of precedents within contexts—was more valuable than a simple insistence on principles as absolutes in themselves. This was valuable for jurisprudence and for medicine, the disciplines in which

Avicenna and Averroes were active, and also had far-reaching effects in public life, in the relationship of state to citizen, and religious authority to the individual.

Following Aristotle, Avicenna makes the distinction between the sphere of essence or Form and the sphere of existence or matter. All creation is, necessarily and for eternity, dependent upon God. But the human rational soul mediates between essence and existence. It asserts its own existence consciously, as when it says 'I am'. By so doing, man not only affirms the existence of his soul, but also his free will and thus his power to act and change according to his ethics, which was man's way of reading the mind of God, and of intervening in this 'marvellous order of being'. This was a Neoplatonist synthesis in a line of descent from Plotinus.

Aristotle taught, in his *De Anima* ('On the Soul'), that thinking, like everything else, has a dual aspect: one of the nature of matter, therefore undeveloped, 'passive intellect', and the other of the nature of Form, therefore superior, 'active intellect'. To Avicenna and his heirs in what may be called Aristotle's Arab afterlife, it was clear that the masses represented the 'passive intellect' while they themselves, the philosophers, represented the 'active intellect'. Thus, those of undeveloped intellect require the consolations of religion—and indeed, Avicenna argues, the primary aim of religion is to ensure the happiness of the greatest number: thus he allows to divine revelation a moral and political role. But since those of superior intellect can achieve a greater happiness, these few gifted individuals must pursue a special kind of life dedicated to the speculative pursuit of the highest knowledge.

What is additionally implied is that the God of the philosophers is a God of latitude and generosity, permitting his creatures a considerable measure of independent judgement. The very fact that the philosopher could address revelation and claim to draw variable conclusions as to its purposes was revolutionary—for by this gesture, Avicenna challenged the monopoly of the *qadis* and the *ulema*. One of the main instruments of this Islamic Aufklärung, the application of interpretive reason called *ijtihad*, sorely needs to be revived in Islam today. The God of Avicenna and Averroes certainly favours *sapiens* over *credens*.

Opposition to the *falasifa* was quick to come from Muslim thinkers devoted to the conception of an omniscient and omnipotent God, such as the Baghdad mystic al-Ghazali (Algazel, 1058–1111 CE), who set out to refute Avicenna vehemently in his *Incoherence of the Philosophers*. Algazel articulated the uncompromising stance that the tolerant God of the philosophers could not be the God of Islam. His work was a frontal attack on philosophy *per se*, which he saw as being intractably at odds with the fundamental revelations of the Koran. Algazel accorded to the mystics a higher rank than the *falasifa* among the seekers of Truth. To understand how far the contemporary fundamentalists are from the tradition of Islamic thought, it might suffice to point out that even al-Ghazali is now widely derided as a heretic amongst them.

These disputes would come to a head in al-Andalus, for close to eight centuries the Iberian home of Muslims, Christians and Jews. Avicenna's successor was the epochal figure of Averroes (Ibn Rushd, born 1126 in Cordoba), who further replenished these ideas that were to gush through the dry courses of Christian thought, and provoke into existence a new and critical claim on truth. Averroes would take the criticism of authority even further, asserting that it was the prerogative of the philosopher—and not the jurist or the theologian—to establish the true inner meaning of religious beliefs. But the inspiring story of how a Muslim Andalusian thinker became the teacher of the first anti-dogmatic school of philosophy in Christian Europe remains to be told, in the sub-chapter 'The Faith Party vs. the Reason Party'.

Unwilling to give the perceived adversary more of a due than absolutely necessary, European historical accounts usually reduce these Islamic accomplishments to the safeguarding and forwarding of 'our' treasures. This smug belief overlooks the fact that the savage in the bogs of Middle England was far removed from the supposed heritage of classical antiquity, both in space and sophistication, while the trader in the Baghdad *souk* was a neighbour to Hellas. 'The Arab, almost as much as the Byzantine, was an heir of Graeco-Roman civilisation. His way of life was not very different. A Byzantine felt far more at home in Cairo or Baghdad than he would feel at Paris or Goslar, or even at Rome' (Runciman 1951, Vol. 1: 75). Early Islamic civilisation was not a cold storage for perishables that could not be entrusted to the illiterate barbarians who were then rampaging across Europe, but a factory humming with a variety of technologies and cultural developments. Amongst the many factories that were active—Baghdad, Damascus, Alexandria—none were more impressive and beautifully enduring than the cities of al-Andalus.

THE MEDITERRANEAN CRADLE

For a Song and a Dance

> *I've made this rhyme completely free*
> *of sense—it's not about you or me,*
> *or love, or doings he-and-she,*
> *or springtime thoughts.*
> *It came to me while I was sleeping*
> *on my horse.*

He was a strange boy, the boy who had grown up with fairies. They could never leave the precincts of his castle, but they could always transport themselves back, on flights of song and story, to the paradise they had come from: the paradise that lay beyond the mountains to the south. The fairies took him along on these journeys. They had taught him to sing and play stringed instruments that no one in his homeland had seen before, to compose beautiful poems and prepare his heart for love. By the time he came of age, he had, like many of his aristocratic contemporaries, been trained in the crafts of war and rapine. But he could do more. He could craft verses that praised beauty, the seasons and his idealised love, yet also mock the conceits of the rhymesmith, his language weaving easily between the immediacy of the vernacular tongue and the elegance of metric structure. William IX, Duke of Aquitaine and Count of Poitiers (1071–1127 CE) was to become the first troubadour, the first high poet of modern Europe. His poems are still recited, set to music, taught at university, and invoked by composers active on the world music scene. He embodies the first great burst of creative energy in the European lyric since the waning of Latin poetry. As such, in many academic accounts, he stands alone, an original without teacher or precedent. Hardly anyone remembers the fairies.

In fact, the troubadour tradition, characterised as Christian Europe's very own school of courtly love poetry and music, was ignited by a military skirmish. One of the many campaigns that took William IX's father, William VIII of Aquitaine, into the borderlands of the Pyrenees, between the Christian kingdoms in the south-west of France and northern Spain, whose towns had been transformed by the elegances that the Arabs had brought to this Roman province, when they conquered it from its Visigoth rulers early in the 8th century. Its southern part, Vandalia, had been synonymous with the barbarism of an earlier wave of settlers, the Vandals. In its Arabised form, al-Andalus, this region would sustain Europe's leading culture through the Middle Ages. Muslims, Jews and Christians participated in a rich confluence of religious, literary, musical, scientific, gastronomic and architectural impulses that was to have a lasting impact on European modernity.

> *What planet ruled when I was born?*
> *I'm native here and still I'm foreign.*
> *I'm never at ease and never forlorn,*
> *What can I do?*
> *I was the midnight work of fairies,*
> *The stars danced while I grew.*

William Senior conquered and looted several border towns, among them Barbastro, before deciding to go home. His troops carried away an abundance of riches, but their most prized booty was a caravan of several hundred *qiyan*. In an age when knights measured their victories in terms of goods seized, slaves acquired and lands annexed, the *qiyan* were a treasure of a very different order: chosen for their youth and charm, they were the geishas of al-Andalus; accomplished female entertainers of the elite, singers, dancers and poets, adept in the arts and manners of Andalusian culture, versed in forms such as the Arabic *muwashshaha* and the Jewish *zajal*. They must have truly seemed like fairies of delight to the war-hardened knights, and their presence certainly elevated life at the court of Aquitaine.

William IX grew up amongst these *qiyan*, learning from them Andalusian poems and songs. When he married Philippa of Aragon, his entertainment entourage was further enlarged. 'If singing girls in the 11th century were still expected to have "a repertoire of upwards of 4000 songs, each of them 2 or 4 verses", then one can imagine the influence which several hundred of these girls must have exerted on the society of the Languedoc. The talents of these girls were also much appreciated in the courts of Castile, Aragon and Navarre' (Boase, in Jayyusi 1994, 466). In writing his first airs, William IX studiously followed these role models, and his great theme, that was to define the Troubadour quest, was the same as that of the Sufi poets of the Islamic world: love as a path toward the refinement of the soul and a celebration of the communion between seeker and Sought, rendered through the imagery of an unrequited longing for the Beloved.

Although Islamic theology inclines to the austere, the first centuries of Islamic culture brought into poetry an amazing vigour and diversity. The Arabic poets sang of wine and the Divine, sometimes in the same breath: they used the language of the streets to mark a path towards the sky;

they provoked the authorities and expanded the scope of the sayable. In other words, they were the first Troubadours. Poets like the famed Abu Nuwas and al-Mutanabbi liberated verse from classical restraint by using everyday language and insisting on a dizzying choreography of rhyme. They recast the traditional *qasida*, or ode, in a freer and more personal voice. The wine songs of Abu Nuwas' generation prefigured the *muwashshaha*, the 'ring songs' or 'sash songs', that the *qiyan* taught the young William and his circle of friends. In 1022, half a century before William IX was born, the Andalusian vizier, poet and philosopher Ibn Hazm (994–1064 CE) wrote *The Ring of the Dove*, a treatise elaborating a poetic code of love that is chivalric rather than erotic, a work that should be hailed as the first masterpiece of troubadour poetics. For the first time, the highly sophisticated Romantic love left the high walls of the castles and citadels and mingled with the common folk, entering the repertoire of minstrels and jongleurs. Love tribunals featured song, poetry and judgement according to the 31 articles of the codex of love later recorded in *De Arte Honeste Amandi* by Andreas Capellanus, which was in turn inspired by Ibn Hazm's *Ring of the Dove*: *How often has the miser opened his purse-strings, the scowler unknitted his brow, the coward leapt heroically into the fray, the clod grown sharp-witted (...) and all because of love!* The legacies of Abu Nuwas, of Ibn Hazm, and of the *qiyan* were to be decisive in the development of the troubadour aesthetic, with its emphasis on a chaste courtly love, the object of its tender attention usually a woman who is unattainable.

> *My lady's face I have never seen:*
> *I don't know if she's sweet or serene,*

> *or if she's kind to me or mean.*
> *Why should I care?*
> *So long as the Normans go away*
> *before night falls here.*

In the conception of love that the Arabic poets celebrated, and which the Troubadours would pursue, the Beloved is regarded as sovereign and perfect while the lover must be faithful and submissive. His devotion must be nourished in secret and alluded to only through asides, riddles and clues. Such a love can ennoble but also destroy, and the poet-lover must walk this hazardous razor's edge, 'living dangerously', in Nietzsche's phrase. The Sufis of Baghdad and the Minnesänger of the Wartburg have quenched their passion at the same fountain, sharing aesthetic and spiritual inclinations so closely that the question 'How could the West have conversed with the East?' is rendered nonsensical. Rather, it is impossible to determine where the Orient ends and the Occident begins.

> *This verse I've made—of what or who*
> *unknown—I'll send to someone who*
> *will send it on to someone who*
> *is in Anjou,*
> *who might decode it and convey*
> *the key to you.*

But, as these four stanzas from the most famous of William IX's poems, *Farai un vers de dreyt nien* shows, there is another, dramatic influence. The surreal playfulness, the elusiveness and alertness, the catch-me-if-you-can, topsy-turvy quality are well-known instruments of enlightenment in the East, already present in Sanskrit poetry and story cycles as well as in the allegories and anecdotes of Sufism. At some point in the beginning of the new millennium, the Ship of Fools docked in Europe, carrying a cargo of substantial 'nonsense'.

William IX's influence was amplified by the fact that his granddaughter became Europe's most powerful woman and most active patron of the Troubadours. Eleanor of Aquitaine was queen consort, first of Louis VII of France and then of Henry II of England, and mother of Richard the Lion-Heart. She transformed the court of Poitiers into a Mecca of poetry and a model of courtly sensibilities.

Of course, the Troubadours who congregated in Poitiers were also influenced by Latin poetry like Ovid's *Ars Amatoria* and by local folklore like the Celtic fairytales. But, nomen est omen: the very word that defined them was of Arab origin. Some academic speculators have struggled to derive it from the Occitanian *trobar*, to find, which unwittingly implies that they found a treasure at the end of the rainbow. But authorities like the mythologist Joseph Campbell in *The Masks of God* and Idries Shah in *The Sufis* trace the word far more convincingly to the Arabic root *TRB*. To this day, the verb *TaRaB*—'to sing, to play music; to be moved by joy or grief; to fill with delight'—is one of the key terms in Arabic music, and *-ador* is simply the Provencal suffix of agency (also evident in the title of that diametrically opposed figure, the conquistador).

Thus '*TaRaB*-ador' speaks of the twin forces of influence and innovation, for these early European singers cast aside the dead letter of the Latin they had been taught by their monkish tutors, choosing to follow the fairies, with open ears, into the street and the marketplace, onto the mule track and the pilgrim route, soaking up the vernaculars. Celebrating Provencal and Galician, Mozarabic and *langue d'oc*, the troubadours defied the scriptural authority of Latin as they began to explore new territories in defiance of the suspicious scrutiny of the Church. *TaRaB*, in Christian Europe, spelled the birth of a secular vision of art.

∞

In a culture where a man could inhale in one language and exhale in another, where he played one role for one set of people at dawn and another for another at noon, where he sat in court six days of the week and in the court of God on the seventh day, worked to perfect himself with the quill as well as the sabre, one name was not enough to carry the weight of his ambitions and achievements. His given name was Ishmail in his native Arabic, the language his family spoke at home; in Hebrew, his ancestral language, he was called Shmuel (Samuel). In the circle of his coreligionists, he bore the patronymic of ha-Levi ben Josef; in public documents, he was described as Ibn Nagrila. When he rose to become, at the early age of 34, head of the Jewish community in his city-state, he was styled ha-Nagid, 'the prince'. Born in 993 to a prosperous spice merchant in what was still the Umayyad Caliphate of al-Qurtuba, today's Cordoba, Samuel ha-Nagid was one of the great success stories of al-Andalus. Beginning as a merchant, he soon went to work as a scribe and secretary for the vizier of Granada, composing such eloquent and meticulously wrought letters for him that the emir soon realised there was a more gifted hand at work. He discovered Samuel in the secretariat, and not too many years later, Samuel was appointed vizier himself.

Religious identities are so sharply polarised in our time, and we are so far away from the openness of al-Andalus, that we find it difficult to imagine how this resourceful and talented Jew could have remained the second most powerful man in a Muslim kingdom until his death in 1056. We cannot imagine how a rabbinical scholar could have led the emir's armies into battle, presiding over three notable triumphs: in 1038 over Almeria, in 1039 over Seville, and in 1041, the third and most crucial battle, over the rebellious forces of the emir's cousin. As a general, he composed prayers of thanksgiving for the victory of his Muslim soldiers. As a Rabbi, he made endowments to Judaic religious institutions and paid for the upkeep of shrines in Jerusalem. And yet he expressed himself in Arabic and the Romance vernacular, the mother tongues shared by all communities in al-Andalus. Although schooled both in the Bible and Talmud as well as in the Quran and Islamic jurisprudence—during his period, Jews and Muslims could even study together under the same teachers—this exalted courtier must surely have suffered a sense of sorrow at the stagnation into which his ancestral language had fallen. Hebrew had been confined to the synagogue for a thousand years; it was not the tongue in which Andalusian Jews argued, traded, courted, made love and rejoiced. But Samuel was a visionary. Surrounded by the aesthetic grandeur of Arabic poetry, he felt called upon to rescue Hebrew from the liturgy and equip it to course through the canals of everyday life and the streams of secular poetry.

He used Arabic as his model, of course, adapting both its metrical structures and its freedom with vernacular usage: his syllables expanded and contracted along the breath pattern of a quantitative prosody. As a poet, one of the greatest of the Andalusian poets, Samuel wrote about love and friendship, wine and the gifts of geography and the seasons; he composed eulogies to his patron, the ruler, and he summed up the wisdom of the ages in aphorisms.

Samuel's greatest discovery, perhaps, came to him when he was casting about for appropriate models for a Hebrew renewed for everyday life. Something he had known all his life now struck him with the force of an epiphany: all Andalusians of cultivated taste, whether Muslim or Jewish, could recite pre-Islamic Arabic love poems; Arabic was a language capacious enough to contain a spectrum of themes, tonalities and emotional interests. Muslim piety, being confident and secure in its sense of being rightly guided, did not feel insecure in the face of this-worldly concerns. Why could the architecture of Hebrew not, similarly, be enlarged to encompass more than the narrow house of prayer? Why could it not speak of the world of the senses, of human perceptions and sentiments? In answering these questions, in thought and poetic practice, he endowed the sacred with sensual immediacy and the secular with holiness. Now Samuel and his successors could see the Bible itself with freshly opened eyes, so that the Song of Solomon—which perplexes the puritanical even today—appeared as a paean to frank and passionate pleasure. Sometimes, a borrowed voice sets the true one free.

Samuel's innovations put an important principle of literary practice into play: that the fossil fuels of scriptural language could not take precedence over the renewable resources of everyday conversation, with its mercurial shifts of phrase and tone, its appetite for a spoken music. Just as importantly, and perhaps without anticipating such a consequence, they heralded a revolutionary political idea, which would resonate far beyond the Jewish communities of Granada, Seville and Saragossa—namely, that the imagination should never consent to being the servant of sacred authority, but should always embrace the plenitude of secular experience. Not irrelevantly, the Greek root of the word 'heresy', the epithet with which Christian Europe greeted many of the more disconcerting intellectual gifts of the Islamic Mediterranean, is *heresis*: choice.

DJ Boccaccio and the Great 14th Century Remix

To the courtiers and ladies of Norman England, who knew of books largely through hearsay, he was a savant without parallel, who spoke familiarly and with enthusiasm about marvels they had never heard of before. He told them about cities where one could walk safely at night on paved streets lit by street lamps, about palaces for the sick, about tamed forests where the flowers blossomed into ornaments and the waters soared up like spires. He amazed them with astrolabes, intricately constructed instruments that allowed for accurate measurements out on the high seas, and he calculated calendars for them. When they suffered severe pain, he prescribed mandrake. And during the long winter evenings, he entertained them with fanciful tales of travellers and magicians, knights and monsters, tutored them gently with parables of morality and civilised conduct.

Petrus Alfonsi was a convert. Born a Jew in al-Andalus in 1066, he had received the education customary for a member of the cultivated Muslim-Jewish elite. At the age of 40, he was baptised in a highly public ceremony presided over by his patron, King Alfonso I of Aragon. In the process, he seems to have alienated himself from family and community. He left his Spanish homeland to journey north, going first to Normandy and then to England. There, he must have felt like the one-eyed man in the land of the blind. The education he had received back home placed him in a position of great advantage in a society that was, in scientific as well as in literary matters, decidedly primitive. Petrus made the most of the situation. He became a physician at the court of Henry I, and also its leading resident man of wisdom. Publishing on a variety of learned subjects, he soon achieved literary fame. His books were widely read in England and translated throughout Christian Europe; they were the 'bestsellers' of their times. His writings are mostly forgotten, with the exception of his single work of fiction, published in 1115. Titled *Disciplina Clericalis (Tales of the Priest)*, this was an anthology of 34 stories, translated from the Arabic into Latin: a small and representative selection from the vast reservoir of stories to which he was heir, but impressive enough to excite generations of readers and listeners in Christian Europe. For this was the first story-collection of Latin literature in the Middle Ages.

These stories were drawn from an ocean of fables, parables, allegories and adventures. Most famous of all is the Arabic *Alf Laila wa Laila*, the *Thousand and One Nights*. But there are precedents: for one, the Sanskrit *Vetala-pancavimsati*, the 'Twenty-five Tales of the Vampire'. There was also the *Katha-sarit-sagar*, the 'Ocean of the Rivers of Stories', originally composed in the Paishachi tongue in Kashmir, and above all, there was the Sanskrit *Panchatantra*, which had travelled westward in numerous disguises, appearing in Persian and

Arabic as the *Dastan Kalilah wa Dimnah*. This 8th-century translation made in Baghdad was then conveyed into Syriac, Greek, Hebrew and Latin, and eventually—through the efforts of Petrus and the raconteurs who succeeded him—infused even the Welsh and French repertories of narrative. La Fontaine paid it explicit homage in the introduction to the second volume of his *Fables* (1678).

Petrus' narratives were bursting with tall tales and curiosities, audacious exaggerations and caveats pressed home, figures from the daily life of castle, cottage and field, as well as alchemists and sorcerers from beyond the horizons of the known. But how were these stories to be held together, Petrus Alfonsi must have asked himself. The solution was near at hand. He had grown up in the tradition of the frame story, where one narrative was nested inside another, each ivory box opening to reveal yet another, smaller and more exquisite. For the skilled storyteller in the 'Oriental bazaar' was hardly the naïve fairy-teller often made out to be, but a highly-skilled manipulator of suspense and psychology.

All the great story collections mentioned above operate on this principle. That is also how Petrus Alfonsi intertwined his stories with the conversation between a father and a son serving as a frame. That is how the stories are introduced in the *Panchatantra*—a sage named Vishnu Sharman is asked to counsel five young princes, to instruct them in the manners of the world and about how to survive in this tricky world. The sage starts telling them of two jackals that meet in a forest, endearing rogues who tweak each others' tails with tall stories. That is exactly how the very first West European fiction writers organised their imaginary material: Boccaccio's *Decameron* and Chaucer's *Canterbury Tales*, the two most influential prose works of the Renaissance, fountainheads of a vast literary sea. Nothing like this had previously existed in Latin literature. 'Christian texts were pretty much all the Latin literature that anyone had read or studied ... for a very long time. But Arabic brought with it treasures that had little to do with religion ...' (Menocal 2002, 75). All the central aspects of these two epochal works are familiar to a literary traveller: the story in a story in a story, a trick box similar to the Russian babushkas; the idea of a story-telling contest, whether to pass time, as in Chaucer, or to survive a deadly threat, as in Boccaccio. As raconteurs, the pilgrims journeying to Canterbury and the Florentine *jeunesse dorée* are descendants of Vishnu Sharman and Scheherazade.

But the close similarities do not end with the structure. The stories themselves are retellings of a narrative heritage that goes all the way back to ancient India. Boccaccio reads like a DJ who is remixing evergreens: the second tale of the second day, the loss and recovery of Rinaldo's property, is from the *Panchatantra*, as is the second tale of the third day, in which the tactful King Agilulf matches wits with the groom who has seduced his Queen, a charming story from the *Panchatantra* that is beloved throughout India even today. In the fifth tale of the third day, Zima, a young man infatuated with a married lady, offers her husband his beautiful horse in exchange for a few words with her. The wily aristocrat accepts the deal, urging his wife not to give any reply. She obeys, but the beauty of Zima's love declaration sways her, as does his cleverness, for when she remains silent, he answers on her behalf, and so manages to arrange a first rendezvous with her. This tale is from the *Hitopadesha* (Sanskrit: 'The Instruction in Well-Being'), a parallel to the *Panchatantra* that was translated into Arabic and Persian, from where it entered a collection titled *The Fables of Sinbad*, widely circulated in Latin at the time of the Florentine master. The ninth tale of the third day, which tells of the vexed love between Gilette and Bertrand, is based on one of the greatest of the Sanskrit plays, Kalidasa's *The Recognition of Sakuntala*, available at the time in an 11th-century French version. On the fourth day, Boccaccio breaks the pattern, offering a defence of his work by telling a story himself, of the hermit Filipo Balducci and his son. At the age of 18, the son leaves the retreat and enters the city, where he is fascinated with the female. This story originates in a legend nested within the great Indian epic *Ramayana*, where the lad is called Rishyashringa, which means 'the young sage with the single horn'. Incidentally, this is the origin of the topos of 'The Virgin and the Unicorn', well known in Christian legend and iconography; it also fed into the Andalusian Ibn Tufayl's philosophical allegory, *Hayy Ibn Yaqzan* ('Alive, Son of Awake'), whose hero is reared by a gazelle and grows to manhood on a desert island (see the sub-chapter 'The Faith Party vs. the Reason Party').

The second tale of the fourth day, in which a lusty friar insinuates himself into a lady's bed as the archangel Gabriel, is a wonderful example of how such stories flowed from the *Panchatantra* (where the angel is the demigod Indra) through the *Thousand and One Nights* to European collections. The first tale of the fifth day leads us back in time into Buddhist lore. The story of the two young Cypriots, who brave adversity to win their brides, appears in *Barlaam and Josaphat*, an 8th-century Greek Christianisation of the life of the Buddha and the stories of his previous births.

The translator was none other than St John of Damascus, a leading figure in Umayyad Christianity. These stories circulated so widely and became so popular—they were also current in an Arabic version, *Bilawar and Buddhasaf*—that Josaphat (a well-attested corruption of Bodhisattva) was 'canonised by the 14th century, and worshipped as a saint in the Catholic Church', as was Barlaam (Skilton 1994, 199). It is a comforting thought that a Christian praying to St Josaphat on his feast day of 27 November is also invoking the grace of the Compassionate One.

Several dozen of Boccaccio's one hundred and one stories can be traced to Eastern predecessors. Petrus Alfonsi's *Disciplina Clericalis* was by no means the only popular import. The Middle Ages were very fertile in myth and legend. Jewish authors also participated in the vast sowing of Oriental lore in the West. Standard Arabic collections were translated into Hebrew and from there into Latin. The *Panchatantra* for example, repackaged as *The Fables of Bidpai*, went through an 8th-century Arabic version and a Hebrew rendering before it became, in the 12th century, John of Capua's *Directorium humanae vitae* ('Guide for Human Life'), one of the most celebrated rosaries of moralistic tales.

Both in their exotic content and the novel manner of their telling, Boccaccio and Chaucer revolutionised literature in Christian Europe. Petrus' little stories would be told and retold, adapted and embellished. Caxton's version of Aesop's fables contained many Alfonsi stories, as did the *Gesta Romanorum*, which was to inspire generations of European writers, even contributing plot elements to the plays of Shakespeare and Marlowe. At the end of the day, the convert had converted those who converted him, to the culture that he had deliberately left behind.

Unfortunately, *Tales of the Priest* was not Alfonsi's only mark on the future. His diatribe, *A Dialogue against the Jews*, remained in circulation long after he had passed away. Its title is misleading, for it is a polemic, not a dialogue, and one aimed against both Judaism and Islam. Accurate as it is, in its exposition of the tenets of both religions, it denounces them in bitter and vituperative terms: it served anti-Jewish and anti-Muslim propagandists as a major source in later years, all the more authoritative for having been authored by a convert who had seen the light of the Church and mended the error of his birth. And so, in the ambivalent figure of Petrus Alfonsi, we find interwoven two opposed strands that would shape Europe: the marvellous wealth of secular narrative, on the one hand, and the demonic inheritance of anti-Semitism and anti-Islamism on the other.

Dante Between Heaven and Hell

If European literature is a city, Dante's *Divina Commedia* is its cathedral. Stepping in, we marvel at the Christian frescoes adorning its walls and ceiling. The chandeliers, medallions and other adornments take us back into the Roman past. And from the portraits in the niches, an assembly of contemporaries and ancestors observe us balefully. The dome of the *Divina Commedia* is breathtakingly high, the structure with its three wings imposing. A lasting monument to Christendom's spiritual glory, our learned guide proclaims, a story of how the soul finds healing and transcendence by journeying to hell and heaven. A saga both historically specific as well as allegorical, told in a voice heard for the first time, the voice of humanism speaking in the language of everyday life. It marks the conclusion of the Mediaeval and the beginning of the Renaissance.

But afterwards, having admired everything at length and leisure, suitably inspired and transported, we stand in the piazza and look back at the contours of this edifice—and are struck by a sense of déjà vu. The account of this odyssey through Hell, Purgatory and Paradise, so uncommon to Christian myth, was not new at the time of its Italian rendering.

A man of special gifts is awoken at night by an angel and carried up to heaven. The man rides a winged horse, ascending nine circles, a long journey broken by a series of way-stations, in an Otherworld of confusing strangeness, meeting prophets and men of stature. Above the ninth circle he finally finds himself in the presence of God. But that was only one part of his journey. After encountering the terrifying guardian angel of Hell, the traveller is brought face to face with the circles of the Damned, with the sins that called down their punishment and the torments they are condemned to. This terrifying Inferno funnels away into the depths of eternal despair.

The man is the prophet Mohammed, and this story has been told and retold as an apocryphal but very powerful fable throughout the Muslim world since the 8th century. Called *al-Mir'aj*, 'the Ascent', it is known in many variations, some of them baroque in detail, some of them Romanesquely austere, and has inflamed the imagination of many Ottoman and Safavid painters (interestingly, most of the extant portraits of the Prophet depict him during the *mir'aj*). By the time this vision of multiple heavens and hells reached the Mediterranean, it was already a rich tapestry of many influences. The ultimate origin probably lies in the vivid celestial and infernal *mandalas* of Hinduism and later Buddhism, which would have flowed into Islamic culture through the Barmecide-sponsored translations in Abbasid Baghdad. This folklore inspired the devotional visions of the greatest of Sufi mystics, Ibn al-Arabi and al-Ma'ari. Ibn al-Arabi (1165–1240) was a native of Murcia in southern Spain, and in the 12 volumes of his magnum opus, *The Meccan Revelations*, he explored a revolutionary path to the Divine. 'The infernal regions, the astronomical heavens, the circles of the mystic rose, the choirs of angels around the focus of divine light, the three circles symbolising the Trinity—all are described by Dante exactly as Ibn al-Arabi described them,' writes R. A. Nicholson. 'It may be added that Ibn al-Arabi too had a Beatrice—Nizam, the beautiful and accomplished daughter of Makinu'ddin.... In short, the parallelism, both general and particular, reaches so far that only one conclusion is possible. Muslim religious legends ... must have passed into the common stock of literary culture that was accessible to the best minds in Europe in the 13th century' (quoted in Campbell 1968, 129–30).

The similarities do not end there. They pile up when we compare the architecture of heaven and hell in the Mir'aj stories and in the *Commedia*, which Dante began in 1308 and completed shortly before his death in 1321. Both texts invoke images of light, symbols of circularity, and the interplay of blindness and revelation. The Prophet finds his eyesight darkening over and fears that he will be blinded by the light that overwhelms him at every new stage of his celestial ascent, only to realise that his eyes have been prepared for special vision, just like Dante after him. Gabriel takes him in hand, as guide, comforter and intercessor with God, offering him theological explanations, just as Virgil does with Dante. The Prophet is delighted by the choirs and heavenly harmonies that greet him, and awed by the concentric hierarchies of angels circling the Throne of God, just as Dante, too, was to be. The Prophet is horrified to meet the guardian angel of Hell, and at the vision of eternal damnation that is unveiled during his infernal descent. As Dante is later to do, the Prophet declares himself incapable of describing his experience, recalling it only as a sort of 'ineffable suspension of the soul', communicable only in the tenor of dreamlike allegory. Most obvious are the similarities regarding some of the punishments: the black storm on the adulteress, the rain of fire on the sodomites, which forces them to march in circles, the suffering of the soothsayers, whose heads are twisted around on their necks, the schismatics who are stabbed without ever dying, the giants whose vastness is described with equally metric precision, the vision of Lucifer trapped in ice exactly like the Islamic Iblis, the cleansing in the two rivers of the earthly paradise, and so on and so forth. 'When we summarise all the analogies in structure, topography and plot, it becomes clear that one single religious text, an Islamic one at that, resembles Dante's work more closely—in its themes, in its eschatology, in ideas, imagery, symbols and descriptions— than all the other religious texts put together, which Dante scholars use to explain the genesis of the *Divina Commedia*' (Asin y Palacios 1923).

But how did Dante become aware of this Islamic legend? A Mir'aj version had appeared as an addendum to the

Historia Arabum (1256), the first history of the Arab world in Latin, written by the Archbishop of Toledo, Rodrigo Jimenez de Rada—five years before Dante was born, and four years before the poet's teacher and acknowledged master Brunetto Latini (1210–1294) came to Toledo as the ambassador of the Florentine Republic to the court of Alfonso X of Castile and Leon, known as 'the Wise'. We can easily imagine the impression that this grand Hispano-Arab capital—regarded as the pinnacle of learning of its time, where it was quite normal to interweave elements from the antique Greek, Christian and Muslim streams, whether in literature, science or philosophy—would have made on Latini. For he was not only a notary and a diplomat, but also an intellectual who wrote one of the first manuals of rhetoric for a European vernacular, and mentor to Dante's generation of politically hyperactive, widely curious and intellectually agile Florentines. In 1264, the Toledo school of translation rendered an authoritative Mir'aj version into Latin. This work, which embodied a synthesis of Islamic mysticism and Neoplatonism, soon appeared in Latin and French, and in Italian as the *Libro della Scala*, 'The Book of the Ladder', and found its way into the libraries of cultivated Italian intellectuals.

Indeed, Islamic influences were so pervasive that it would be far more difficult to prove that Dante was ignorant of them, than that he was familiar with them. All Dante scholars have underlined his universal curiosity, one of the major intellectual qualities of the Renaissance man. In his other writings, he often refers to the Arab astronomers Albumazar, Alfraganius and Alpetragius, and the philosophers Alfarabius, Algazel, Avicenna and

Averroes. The debate over faith and reason among the last three named was the foundation on which Pierre Abelard, Roger Bacon and Siger of Brabant raised the movement of Averroist Scholasticism—with which Dante was intimately familiar (several of the figures from this cast of characters, both Muslim and Christian, appear in the *Commedia*).

But nowhere does Dante acknowledge any precursors of the *Commedia*. His silences express a literary and religious anxiety, as an Italian scholar insightfully writes: 'One sees how Dante passes over his more troublesome predecessors in silence: Giacomino da Verona, who, though a mediocre poet, had already conceived the idea of describing the Christian hereafter, and therefore cast a shadow on Dante's glory; the Arab poets, whom he knew through Brunetto Latini—a precise knowledge he carefully disguised for other reasons (a sacred poem of Christianity inspired by the paradisaical visions of Muslim poets!). Plato had said in *Phaedrus* that the vision and description of the empyrean are beyond human powers. This declaration does not hold true for Dante, however, the only one who has succeeded in such a venture. And this is the reason why he does not encounter a single poet, classic or contemporary, in paradise. He stands alone, the "Emperor's" unvanquished champion' (Ferrucci 1980, 96).

Evidently, he felt that making a bow towards his exemplars would have reduced him to an adapter, albeit a brilliant one, rather than an originator. This attitude prevails in Europe until today, an obsession with a pure origin, as if the fact of outside influences would contaminate one's own identity and diminish one's greatness. In our minds, exactly the opposite is true. The achievement of a colossal figure like Dante is that he was receptive to pre-existing ideas, and that he had the energy and the vision to form an individual masterpiece in the spirit of confluence. Unfortunately, the denial and erasure of Muslim precursors was about to become a common editorial manoeuvre in theology, literature and science.

Part of this process was the demonisation of Mohammed and sadly enough, Dante falls into the pit of primitivism when describing a degradingly foul punishment for the Prophet:

> *'No cask ever gapes so wide for loss*
> *of mid- or side-stave as the soul I saw*
> *cleft from the chin right down to where men fart.*
> *Between the legs the entrails dangled. I saw*
> *the innards and the loathsome sack*
> *that turns what one has swallowed into shit.*
> *While I was caught up in the sight of him,*
> *he looked at me and, with his hands, ripped apart*
> *his chest, saying: "See how I rend myself,*
> *see how mangled is Mohammed!*
> *Ahead of me proceeds Alì, in tears,*
> *his face split open from his chin to forelock.*
> *And all the others whom you see*
> *sowed scandal and schism while they lived.'*
> *(Inferno, XXVIII, 19ff.)*

By contrast, the poet's teacher—the father figure through whom he had learned of the *Mir'aj* and who had instilled in him the love of the vernacular—got off relatively lightly. Dante incarcerated Brunetto Latini in the third ring of the seventh circle of Hell, the one reserved for sodomites.

Translation is Not Treason

Mysterious are the paths of the manuscripts. Take a Greek treatise for example, inscribed on parchment in Miletus and carried away in a metal cylinder to Alexandria, where it rests a few centuries, before it is donated on a special request by a visiting scholar to the University of Edessa, from where, after serving many inquisitive eyes, it is spirited away to the library of the Abbasid Caliph in Baghdad. There it is chosen, as one of many Greek manuscripts, to be rendered into Arabic by a team of Syrian Christian scholars. The manuscript passes into a new body, made of papyrus and calligraphed in Arabic letters, adorned with beautiful ornaments. Sold to a learned Baghdadi family, this manuscript is one day secreted in an ivory casket, and taken by the son of the house on a business trip, by sea mostly, to Cordoba, at the western end of the Islamic world, and gifted to the Vizier, from whose private collection it passes into the ownership of an Andalusian Jew, several generations later, who translates it into Hebrew, a process that in turn inspires a contemporary of his, a widely travelled Christian originally from the Frankish lands, to render it into Latin in Toledo, on a superior material that has recently been imported from Palermo—paper. In this avatar, the manuscript is sold to the Benedictine monastery of Cluny, whose enlightened abbot is an avid collector of Arab literature. Here it is copied and distributed among the libraries budding in Christian Europe, one of which is in Venice. And when a new technology called printing booms in the city of St Mark, this text is set in lead and multiplied, so that today a copy is available in the Bibliothéque Nationale in Paris, the Staatsbibliothek in Munich and in several other libraries, resting in the rare-books departments, which are air-conditioned to guarantee its longevity, as if it has not survived the ages with tenacity and style.

Knowledge depends upon a critical mass of textual availability. We are so used to the all-encompassing vastness of the book market and the Internet, that it takes an effort to imagine the attraction and wonderment that the libraries and universities of al-Andalus held for Christians. The Caliphal library in Cordoba for instance, one of 70 major libraries in al-Andalus, prided itself on 400,000 books. By contrast, the monastery of St Gall in Switzerland, which possessed one of the leading libraries in Christian Europe at the time, owned 600 manuscripts (Hillenbrand, in Jayyusi 1994, 121). How were the monks going to start a Renaissance with such a meagre handful of books? Not surprisingly, as a historian of science observes, 'Cordoba in particular was an irresistible magnet, attracting many young, well-born Europeans, whose families sent them to the fabled Spanish metropolis to get "finished"' (Turner 1997, 201), in much the same way that students from all over the world now apply to Ivy League universities in the USA. 'In most of the arts and sciences of civilisation, mediaeval Europe was a pupil and in a sense a dependant of the Islamic World, relying on Arabic versions even for many otherwise unknown Greek works' (Lewis 1986, 7).

Toledo, at the heart of La Mancha, once the citadel of the barbarian Visigoths, became the Baghdad of the West: it enjoyed the distinction of hosting Europe's first modern school of translation—the *Escuela de Traductores*—established by Raimundo of Sauvetat, the city's archbishop in the first half of the 12th century. This inaugurated a lively stock exchange where treatises, surveys, anthologies and compendia were traded among languages: treasures that had long been the preserve of Arabic were distributed among the intelligentsia of Christendom. Christian monks, scholars and poets crossed the Pyrenees, or sailed from Italy, to partake of the intellectual feast.

Promising scholars from across Europe were recruited into the ongoing project: foremost among them, Gerard of Cremona, Michael Scot, Robert of Ketton, and Hermannus 'Alemannus' of Carinthia. Thousands of manuscripts were translated: texts began to flow in various directions among Greek, Arabic, Hebrew and Latin, and into the headwaters of the emerging languages of Castilian, Occidental, French and Italian. A special process of collaborative translation, *traduction-à-deux*, was developed: usually a Jew (occasionally a Muslim) translated the Arabic text orally into Romance or Castilian, before a Christian rendered this oral version into written Latin.

Working on a bridge between languages, these Jewish interpreters and Latin scribes translated the Greek originals, and the Arabic commentaries as well as the original works of the Arab masters. One of the most industrious of the Toledo translators, Gerard of Cremona (c. 1114–1187 CE) conveyed into Latin no fewer than 90 works, among them epochal writings of Aristotle, Euclid, Ptolemy, Galen, the Neoplatonists Plotinus and Proclus, as well as al-Kindi, Alfarabius, Avicenna and Averroes. Three of Gerard's translations were to transform the theory and practice of medicine in Christian Europe: Avicenna's *Qanun fi al-Tibb* or *The Canon of Medicine* (a magisterial compendium of Greek, Indian, Arab and Chinese medical knowledge); Albucasis' *At-Tashreef* or *The Method* (a lucid collection of case studies and clinical observations that contains the earliest known description of hemophilia); and the corpus of Galen (the lost writings of this Greek physician were known only through Hunayn ibn Ishaq's 9th-century Arabic translation). These three texts were to serve as the basis for a competent medical education in Christian Europe for the next five centuries. Between 1500 and 1550, more than 30 editions of Avicenna's *Canon* were to be printed in Italy alone. Europe benefited from the applied science of the Arab thinkers: 'Notwithstanding the Muslim concern for preparing for life in the hereafter, Muslim scientific effort, from the very beginning, focused most immediately on gaining knowledge that could be applied in making life better and more efficient on Earth' (Turner 1997, 23).

In 1143, Christian Europe could finally read the Koran. At the urging of Peter the Venerable, abbot of Cluny, Robert of Ketton produced the first Latin translation of Islam's foundational scripture. This was a major step, although the translation—hastily done—was dogged by error, and bundles the text with the Prophet's sayings and an account of his life, and those of the first four Caliphs. Peter the Venerable was a votary of interfaith dialogue, although he camouflaged it under the desire to refute Islam and vindicate Christianity. Even as he published polemics against Judaism and Islam, Peter understood Jews and Muslims to be 'peoples of the Book' in the Prophet's sense, and eventually receivable into Christ's grace. In his epoch, it was politic to couch one's positive interest in the Other in the negative language of defensiveness, lest one be penalised by members of one's own persuasion. A pacifist, Peter had opposed the Crusades, arguing that the Muslims could better be converted 'not as our people often do, by weapons, not by force but by reason, not by hate but by love' (Kritzeck 1964, 161) and his fanatical monastic rival, Bernard of Clairvaux, kept an eagle eye out for his lapses into Islamophilia. Translation, as Peter tried to convince his contemporaries, was not treason, but the gateway to mutual understanding and to the possibility of universal peace.

One of the most remarkable citizens of this remarkable city was Rodrigo Jimenez de Rada, who became its Archbishop in 1209 and held that exalted position until his death in 1247. Fluent in Arabic himself, he was an enthusiastic patron of his city's 'school of translation', and wrote the first Latin history of Islam, the *Historia Arabum*, which we have already encountered in relation to the Mir'aj narratives and Dante. De Rada was one of the earliest Christian scholars to treat Islam as a culture that called for research and understanding, rather than a heresy to be condemned or a rival faith to be struck down. De Rada commissioned Mark, a canon of Toledo, to translate the Koran. Literal and precise, Mark's Koran translation was superior to Ketton's clumsy effort, with its spiteful marginalia.

The *Escuela de Traductores* received help from a new invention. As the legend goes, the Arabs learned paper-making from Chinese technicians captured in a battle in Central Asia. The first paper factory in the Islamic world was set up by the Barmecides in Baghdad in 800 CE, and the technology reached al-Andalus through Sicily two centuries later. The first paper mill in Spain was established at Jativa, followed by paper factories in Toledo. Paper then was made of straw and rice, and increasingly exported to the territories further north. It is highly unlikely that the printing press would have been the success it was, had paper not been in existence.

❧

Michael Scot (c. 1175–c. 1235) was the epitomic Scholar Gypsy. Born in Scotland, this restless savant lived, at various times, in Bologna, Palermo and Toledo; having studied Arabic, he read Ibn Sina and Ibn Rushd in the original and was convinced of his duty to translate them. He also enjoyed the reputation of being a wizard, as a master of astrology, alchemy and the occult sciences. His move from Toledo to Palermo around 1220 was a sign of the shifting metropolitan balance. Together with Hermann der Deutsche, he went to work at the court of Frederick II (1194–1250 CE), the grandson of Roger II, one of the most famous of the 'turbaned kings' or 'baptised sultans' of Sicily. This Arabised Norman monarch was keenly aware that his island territory stood virtually at the centre of Mediterranea: halfway between Europe and Africa, midway between Toledo and Alexandria. As if to celebrate this position of vantage, he commissioned a vast new atlas of the world—which, being dedicated to him by the author, came to be known as the *Kitab al-Rujar* ('The Book of Roger'). The author was al-Idrisi, a Muslim born in Ceuta and educated in Cordoba, who was the first of the Andalusian intellectual fortune-seekers to arrive in Norman Sicily.

When Frederick II came to power, he inherited a library and a laboratory of creative ferment unrivalled in Europe. Called *Stupor Mundi*, 'Wonder of the World', Frederick spoke Arabic, Latin and Occitanian with equal felicity, as though to go with his three titles, for he was King of Jerusalem and Holy Roman Emperor as well as Emperor of Sicily. Scotus and Hermannus brought to his capital, Palermo, a taste for rational intellectual culture that came from working on Greek philosophy and Arab commentary. They were the pillars of an expansive translation industry; in the course of half a century, thousands of volumes were translated into Latin. In 1232, Michael Scot dedicated to the monarch his Latin version of Ibn Sina's treatise, *On Animals*. Meanwhile he had also translated Aristotle's work of the same name, *De Animalibus*, and had overseen, at the royal behest, a fresh and complete translation of Aristotle and his Arab commentators.

In an effort to translate this legacy into a permanent institution of learning, Frederick established the University of Naples in 1224. It was here that the most influential of mediaeval saints, Thomas of Aquinas, was to study theology and philosophy, a decade later, before going to Albertus Magnus in Cologne, and then to Paris, where he joined the war of ideas raging between the Averroists and the Church, a story of epochal consequence told in the next chapter. Giacomo da Lentino, the foremost of Frederick's court poets, experimented with a range of styles before settling on the form of his dreams, the sonnet.

Dante's *Divina Commedia* again serves as a ready reckoner of the way in which these enlightened men were perceived by the bigots: Frederick is banished to the sixth circle of Hell, deposited among heretics who are buried alive in tombs, while Michael Scot's body is contorted, amongst those who are so badly twisted that 'tears from their eyes run down their buttocks and into the cleft' (*further reading not recommended for those under 18*). Devoid of all these great minds, paradise must truly be a boring place.

The Faith Party vs. the Reason Party

In 1175, the Andalusian sage Ibn Tufayl published a philosophical romance, *Hayy Ibn Yaqzan* ('Alive, Son of Awake'), which tells of a boy who is abandoned on a desolate island, reared by a gazelle, and grows to manhood alone. He is not a wild child but a soul chosen for perfection: free from the temptations of the flesh, he develops a *convivencia* with the animals and plants of his habitat, and attains wisdom by the exercise of his inborn faculties of observation and thought. The author balances carefully among reason, faith and mysticism: he demonstrates reason as a God-given faculty and frames his tale with mystical allusions. Hayy climbs, every seven years, to a higher degree of insight into nature, the soul and the Divine. The process continues over seven such seven-year periods, until, at the age of 49, his isolation is ended by a visit from a man from another island. Absal introduces Hayy to language and formal religion; to their delight, they find that their beliefs are identical. Hayy then visits Absal's island, which is ruled by his friend Salaman, but is disappointed that its people are enslaved to sensual pleasures and have scant regard for religion. He is also pained that Salaman interprets religion for his subjects in a simple, literal manner, refusing to stretch their imagination with allegory or inquiry. Hayy speaks to the people about the higher truth, but manages only to confuse and sadden them. Concluding regretfully that wisdom is not for the masses, Hayy retreats with Absal to his uninhabited island, where they spend their lives in meditation and prayer (Bürgel, in Jayyusi 1994, 830–46).

Ibn Tufayl found the thread of his story in one of Ibn Sina's allegories—and it has plausibly been argued that some of its elements come from the same Ramayana legend that, as we have seen, Boccaccio was to knit into his *Decameron*. And *Hayy* itself, travelling through several translations (Moses of Narbonne's Hebrew in 1349, Pococke's Latin of 1671, and Simon Ockley's English of 1708) became a sensation in Europe. It was enthused over by Spinoza, Leibnitz and Locke, and fed into Daniel Defoe's *Robinson Crusoe* (1719). But *Hayy* is not merely a curiosity of intercultural literary history. And, though told with wit and felicity, it is no fairytale either. The Granada-born Ibn Tufayl (1109–1186 CE) was revered as one of the great Arab Aristotelians, in the lineage of al-Kindi, al-Farabi and Ibn Sina.

To his first circle of readers, *Hayy*'s political meaning was manifest: it portrayed his own position as a philosopher in a turbulent society that was coming under the sway of religious absolutism. The rulers of his time, the Almohads, had no love of independent thought, no patience with the philosopher's claim to a higher rung on the ladder of knowledge, and no interest in the Aristotelian teaching that in life every being can strive towards the fulfilment of its *entelechy*, its own potential for perfection. Mystically oriented and militantly intolerant though the Almohads were, they may have appealed to men of reason like Ibn Tufayl as a fresh beginning, an opportunity to direct a fissiparous and self-indulgent society towards the spiritual and political perfection of a Platonic philosopher-king's dreams. Ibn Tufayl's concern with reconciling reason, faith and mysticism, in a close but uneasy relationship with the Almohads, was to provide a model of the intellectual strategies of the Christian philosophers vis-à-vis the dominance of the Catholic Church. Especially through the writings of his protégé, the brilliant Cordoban philosopher, Ibn Rushd (1126–1198).

∝∾

From the 8th to the 15th century, the Islamic world experienced a three-cornered struggle between the Faith Party, the Mysticism Party and the Reason Party. The Faith Party comprised the *ulema* (singular, *alim*, the theologians and jurists), the Mysticism Party consisted of the *auliya* (singular, *wali*, the Sufis) and the Reason Party was constituted by the *falasifa* (singular, *faylasuf*, the philosophers). This struggle had deep roots in the history of Islam, going back to 9th-century Baghdad, when the Abbasid Caliph al-Mamun, founder of the House of Wisdom, had suppressed the Faith Party and championed the Reason Party. Orthodox piety was scandalised by al-Kindi's receptiveness to knowledge irrespective of its religious or cultural sources and by al-Razi's empiricist dismissal of the claims of revelation. The mystics were outraged by al-Farabi's conclusion that the consolations of religion were not sufficient for the philosopher, and Ibn Sina's teaching that philosophers, with their ability to cope with doubt, had a stronger claim to truth than theologians committed to absolutes. The Reason Party's central thesis— that the human mind could comprehend its Creator, and praise or judge among His effects—was anathema to the other two. The balance of authority would shift constantly among these three parties: Faith always occupying the throne, at least nominally, Mysticism wrapping itself in the robe of renown but occasionally provoking suspicion, and Reason acquiring the crown of prestige but periodically attracting repression. A unique feature of this triangle of conflict and coexistence was that all three parties staked a claim on the Divine. Including the philosophers, for they had imbued the teachings of Aristotle with the mother's milk of Plotinus, and were thus strongly influenced by a Neoplatonist preoccupation with the Divine, rather than the more uncompromisingly rationalist Aristotle.

Relations among the parties were complex, as we see in the al-Andalus of the Almohads: marked by wary accommodation at the best of times and vehement hostility at worst, with occasional moments of mutual understanding. All three parties consorted with rulers—because they needed the protection of authority, especially if they were working with potentially inflammatory ideas, and because they saw that being close to the centre of power made it possible for them to influence political and cultural change. Thus, Ibn Tufayl himself served as vizier and court physician to the second Almohad sultan, Abu Yaqub Yusuf (the Salaman of *Hayy Ibn Yaqzan*), and presented Ibn Rushd to this potentate in 1168 CE. Ibn Rushd was immediately named chief *qadi* of Seville, and after Ibn Tufayl's death, succeeded him in his high public offices.

Thus, it is all the more courageous that this great Cordoban philosopher criticised the very regime he served in his *Exposition of the Republic*, in which he placed the Islamic societies of his era under a Platonic lens, observing that although the Islamic ecumene, the *umma*, was a model society in theory, it had in practice degenerated into plutocracy, demagogy and tyranny. Amazingly, the Almohad rulers shielded their stringent resident critic from his enemies, minimising his penalty to temporary exile. To his readers in al-Andalus, and even more crucially, in Christian Europe, as we shall see, Ibn Rushd marked the apogee of Arab Aristotelianism, and made five extraordinary contributions to that philosophical canon.

First, although he made strategic use of Plato's thought, Ibn Rushd broke completely with the Neoplatonist synthesis of theology and philosophy that many of his illustrious predecessors had fashioned in a move to reconcile Faith and Reason. Instead, Ibn Rushd declared forcefully that what is God's must be granted to God and the theologians, and what belongs to temporal and material wisdom must be granted to the philosophers. Second, he emphasised that the ground of all knowledge was the direct, personal experience of reality, and therefore no corpus of unexamined principles could substitute for scientific education and empirical observation. Third, he insisted that the only human antidote to the vagaries of natural contingency is freedom: where freedom is defined as the scope of action of an individual who has acquired moral authority by exercising his will in accord with ethics, logic and science. The exemplar of freedom, for Ibn Rushd, is thus the scholar, the intellectual, the philosopher—who should act as the ultimate arbiter of a society's moral centre and political direction. The philosopher is favoured over the jurist and the theologian in this, because of his intellectual amplitude—his ability to deal with doubt, ambivalence and criticality. Fourth, this gives the philosopher the prerogative to interpret the true meaning of revelation, in the event of a dispute over the apparent and the inner meaning of a scriptural text. And fifth, despite his seeming elitism and pessimism concerning the masses, Ibn Rushd taught that all humans have the potential to nurture their understanding of the cosmos at the levels of theology, philosophy and science—so that all humans, while they have their individual bodied personalities, share a 'unity of the intellect' that is the measure of the Truth invested in their souls.

The world of Islam brushed Ibn Rushd's teachings aside. The Party of Faith and the Party of Mysticism were gaining the ear of power as well as the imagination of the populace. Under the Almohads, the ideal of the 'philosopher-king' was a chimera: the sultan did not relinquish his grip on kingship, and the philosopher could be little more than a vizier with limited powers. But just as Aristotle, lost to Greece, had found an afterlife among the Arabs, so too did Ibn Rushd achieve a dazzling renown among the Christians—especially in Paris, where young scholars had begun to agitate at the barricades against the narrow, censorious and authoritarian approach of the Catholic authorities. To these rebels, Ibn Rushd became the premier symbol of resistance. The real-life Hayy did not retreat to a desert island; he migrated, in spirit, to a land where his doctrines would be alternately celebrated and banned, and used by Christian theologians to settle debates over dogma. He became the battering ram that free thinkers would use in a war of ideas fought out over the 12th and 13th centuries, a war that pitched individual reason against institutional dogma, and would involve the most notable minds of Christian Europe: Pierre Abelard, Albertus Magnus, Roger Bacon, Siger of Brabant and Thomas of Aquinas. All five of these major thinkers regarded their association with Ibn Rushd, whether as disciples or as critics, as fundamental to their work. His Latin admirers displayed his name proudly on their standards, calling themselves Averroists, the 'followers of Ibn Rushd', and their battles transformed the course of European political and cultural history. The script had been rehearsed in Islam; the play would be premiered in Christianity.

∽

In 12th-century Europe, the Church was the Thought Police. The price to be paid for free thinking was a charge of heresy, and the rack, or even the stake. No one could question the clergy, who held the monopoly on truth. The devastating effect on Christian thinking is at hand: between St Augustine and the Averroists lies an intellectual wasteland of seven centuries, relieved only by the occasional scholarly wrangling over musty abstractions. Reality needed to be sawed and stretched to fit the Procrustean bed of revelation. Thus, Christianity's Faith Party regarded the instruments of the Ancients as seditious; while its Reason Party embraced them, in the specific form into which Ibn Rushd had welded them, as indispensable weapons in a liberation struggle.

Among the earliest Christian thinkers to sit at Averroes' feet—and by extension, at the feet of the *faylasuf* lineage— was the radical philosopher, theologian and poet Pierre Abelard (1079–1142 CE). He is mainly remembered, if at all, for his star-crossed love for his pupil, the intelligent and beautiful Heloise: she bore him a son whom they named Astrolabe, being votaries of the new knowledge coming in from the Arab world. But they were forcibly separated. For attending to the voice of love, Abelard was castrated at the order of Heloise's vengeful uncle, a cleric attached to the Cathedral of Paris. And for his philosophical views, which were marked by a degree of candid reformist criticism unimaginable in an authoritarian and sanctimonious religious culture, he was chased from one refuge to another, his work condemned either as presumptuous error or outright heresy: the peripatetic young scholar became a middle-aged fugitive. Abelard was the bravest thinker of his day, and a terror to the orthodox: a believer in the power of natural grace, he refused to treat Christian revelation as a dividing line between the blessed and the damned; he believed that the unbaptised could be redeemed, which made nonsense of the Church's sacraments; he asked how Christian thought could found itself on the writings of pagan and heathen philosophers and then consign them to Hell. While his contemporaries saw Christ's sacrifice as a demonstration to God or the Devil, Abelard insisted it was neither, but an attempt to awaken love in Man, and so win his soul for God.

Abelard's tormentors hated him on many counts: for combining a monastic life with secular disciplines; for listing inconsistencies in the supposedly infallible views of the Church, as recorded through the ages; for reproving monks on their enslavement to habit; for applying the dialectic to the sacred mystery of the Trinity; and for teaching, as the title of his major work puts it, that one can simultaneously say yes *and* no (*Sic et Non*). In words that recall Rhazes' credo against credulity, he declared: 'By doubting, we are led to inquire, by inquiry we perceive the truth.' And more pointedly, aiming his words at the Thought Police of the age: 'The doctors of the Church should be read, not with the necessity to believe, but with liberty to judge' (Campbell 1968, 396–97).

In his last years, Abelard's enemies had him condemned for his demonstration of factual and doctrinal contradictions within the received corpus of Christian theology and history, a condemnation confirmed by Pope Innocent II. When all seemed lost—a lifetime of bitter persecution, narrow escapes, ruinous hurt and disgrace about to end in wrathful punishment—he found sanctuary with Peter the Venerable, the abbot of Cluny and one of the first Christian monks to seek an understanding of Islam and Arab culture. Peter defended Abelard against their worst enemy, the fanatical Bernard of Clairvaux, who regarded himself as the first soldier of the Church of Christ Militant, with a heavenly mission to crush dissent within Christendom and destroy the infidel who had sullied the Holy Lands. Within a generation of Abelard's death, though, the philosopher's influence had become so widespread that the schoolrooms where he had lectured in Paris turned into the Sorbonne, one of the greatest universities in Europe and the seedbed of Averroist Scholasticism.

❧

The University of Paris was a citadel of free thought where the finest minds of Christendom converged in the 12th and 13th centuries. Here, the Averroists lectured on Ibn Rushd's commentaries on Aristotle. Here, they followed the curve of his arguments as they sheared through the theologian's monopoly and established a liberated zone for the philosopher. Trained in the relatively dry dialectical approach to the testing of formulations that Anselm of Canterbury had developed, these Scholastics could barely contain their excitement at receiving nourishment from the Arab Aristotelian heritage. Its procedures and insights carried an unrivalled authority derived not only from intense and fruitful study in the treasure-house of the Greek texts, but also from the fact that this was a philosophy whose exponents had tested its claims in the political arena, at considerable personal risk.

Several generations of Christian intellectuals prospered under the aegis of Ibn Rushd, all the while watched by the Church. Of these, some understood and applied his ideas correctly; others misunderstood and misapplied his thought; and yet others assimilated his vision but deliberately misrepresented it for ideological reasons. Those who embraced Ibn Rushd's doctrines wholly, like Roger Bacon and Siger of Brabant, came under suspicion of heresy, suffered censure and official restraint. Those who subsumed his ideas and then discreetly underplayed him, as Albertus Magnus did—or derogated him, as Thomas of Aquinas did—were treated as favourite sons, rewarded with laudation or high office.

Albertus Magnus (c. 1206–1280) was one of the first Christian scholars to teach that Aristotle and Christianity would have to be reconciled, and that the Arab Aristotelians had shown a way forward, through their own grappling with the parallelism of revelation and reason. While rendering unto theology what was theology's, Albertus was also a scientist who contributed to an array of disciplines, including geography, astronomy, mineralogy and geology. Thomas of Aquinas (1226–1274) was his best student at the Dominican school in Cologne: later known as the 'Angelic Doctor', this theologian and philosopher annotated Aristotle meticulously. And, having digested Ibn Rushd's thought more thoroughly than many of his contemporaries, he proceeded to defend the Church against the Averroist challenge, using a strange collage of misattribution and plagiarism. Roger Bacon

(c. 1214–c. 1294), retrospectively glorified as the 'Miraculous Doctor', was all his life suspected of dabbling in alchemy and the occult. He lectured in Paris between 1237 and 1247, and pursued his interest in logic, mathematics and optics as an independent teacher. Dropping out of sight for a decade, he resurfaced and took vows as a Franciscan monk at some time between 1256 and 1260. His scientific experiments prompted charges of sorcery, especially after he became a monk.

Siger of Brabant (c. 1240–c. 1284), was a brilliant Averroist from the Netherlands who tried to argue his way out of a heresy charge by claiming tactically that Ibn Rushd had taught a doctrine of 'double truth', with faith holding access to the truth of enlightenment and reason opening the gate to the truth of mundane experience. At a deeper level, he believed that the claims of theology and philosophy could never be reconciled: he was the truest follower of Ibn Rushd, in his own eyes and those of his contemporaries Boethius of Dacia and Martin of Denmark, as well as followers like John of Jandun (d. 1328) and Marsilius of Padua (d. 1336 or 1343). These 'Latin Averroists' upheld the idea of a strict philosophy autonomous of theology and applicable not only to physics, medicine and metaphysics, but also to ethical and political questions. This led them to separate the religious and the philosophical as two mutually distinct and exclusive worlds, with emphasis on the latter. They also remained steadfast to the conception, which came to them from Aristotle, through Plotinus and Ibn Rushd, that the soul is bipartite, with an individual part and a divine part; of these, the individual part perishes while the divine part returns to the One. They elaborated Ibn Rushd's theory of the unity of the intellect further, as a potential for perfection that all human beings share. The Church looked upon these ideas with horror: they flew in the face of the official dogma of the immortal individual soul and its resurrection on Judgement Day; they also gave the individual far greater latitude for willed perfection than a system with a monopoly on perfectibility and redemption could tolerate.

All the Christian intellectuals who worked in the shadow of Averroes had benefited from the Latin translations of Aristotle and the classics of Arab Aristotelianism that were pouring in from the Hispano-Arab territories; some of them were more at home in the Andalusian atmosphere of genial collegiality than in the North European ethos of chronic suspicion. All of them emulated Ibn Rushd's spectrum of intellectual interests, being active in theology, philosophy as well as science, or the theory of science. They made no distinction among Christian, pagan and Muslim authorities while arguing questions of Christian doctrine. Indeed, they were far more likely to cite a Muslim thinker than a Patristic writer on central issues of Christian theology. As R. W. Southern writes, 'Western theologians of all shades of opinion in the mid-thirteenth century did not scruple to re-examine traditional views in the light of Islamic philosophy, or at least to restate traditional views in the language of these philosophers' (Southern 1978, 55).

The Church reacted with predictable anxiety when faced with this flow of intellectual riches, forced as it was to acknowledge the enthusiasm with which young Christian scholars—future abbots, archbishops, prelates and even popes—were receiving it. The fearful became terror-mongers; ignorance, exposed, struck back at knowledge with vengeance. The Church responded with the knout of censorship. Through the first half of the 13th century, as it wiped out the mass movement of the Cathars with relentless brutality, the Church cracked down on the dissident scholars of Paris. In 1210, an Episcopal synod decided to ban the study of Ibn Rushd's commentaries on Aristotle at the University of Paris. Five years later, the Church authorities enacted a ban on the study of Aristotle himself. For the rest of the century, Arab Aristotelian thought swung in a penumbral area between prescription and proscription; the more vigorously the Church tried to suppress it, the more dissidents it attracted.

In 1270, Etienne Tempier, Bishop of Paris, condemned two of the theses of the Averroists, following this up seven years later with a 'General Condemnation' of Aristotelianism, listing 219 theses that were declared incompatible with Christian doctrine and placed on the list of prohibited reading. Compiled by a committee of theologians, the list is a comedy of misunderstanding and misattribution: many of the alleged fallacies and heresies had no connection with Aristotle's teaching, or Ibn Rushd's, or with the ideas of the Latin Averroists. The Franciscan Order restrained Roger Bacon from publishing his scientific work without its approval. Fortunately, his acquaintance with Pope Clement IV gave him the necessary respite to compose his *Opus Maius*, concerning the relationship between theology and philosophy. After Clement's death in 1268, he was placed under house arrest for a period, and could never publish again. The statutes of the General Condemnation singled out Siger of Brabant for suppression and summoned him to answer a charge of heresy. He fled the Thought Police, and some time later, word came to his friends that he had been

murdered by a supposed madman—everyone in Paris knew
that he had been silenced. But Siger's radical Averroism, long
outliving him, eventually wove itself into the Renaissance.
And Dante, for once acting without malice, made all
things good in the eyes of the Lord: in *Paradiso*, he sets the
excommunicated Siger of Brabant next to the soon-to-be-
sainted Aquinas in the exalted circle of the Sun.

And the Church—despite its occasional misgivings
about the tenor of his teachings, which once provoked
an investigation into their doctrinal purity—certainly
owed Aquinas his canonisation in 1323. He was the great
champion of the Faith Party against the Party of Reason,
credited with having slain the dragon of Averroism by
refuting its arch-deceit, the doctrine of the 'double truth'—a
doctrine proposed by Siger, not by Ibn Rushd, and then
only to buy himself some breathing space when threatened
with a heresy trial. Ibn Rushd had held that there were two
ways to reach the truth, theology and philosophy, and each
opened up a domain of thought; but not that there were two
truths. So that, when Aquinas upheld the conception of the
'single truth', he was refuting an imaginary Ibn Rushd by
quoting the real Ibn Rushd. Here, as in several other cases,
he appropriated many of Ibn Rushd's ideas and presented
them as refutations of the Cordoban master.

Aquinas modified the Averroist parallelism between
philosophy and theology into a concord between reason and
faith, restoring Ibn Sina's conception of a 'marvellous order
of being'. Aquinas put forward the theory that God has two
aspects: as *Deus revelatus*, He is what He chooses to reveal
of his infinite nature to the finite human understanding; but
as *Deus absconditus*, He is what he chooses to leave hidden

from the understanding. Thus, the intellect must not seek to decipher God's meaning beyond the *revelatus*, and even this understanding can only be achieved through analogy and metaphor. This conception corresponds exactly to Ibn Rushd's teaching that God is both *al-Zahir*, that which is outward and manifest, and *al-Batin*, that which is inward and unrevealed; but for the *faylasuf*, unlike for the Doctor of the Church, the activity of contemplation, interpretation, inquiry and allegorical reading is a route by which the intellect may pass from *al-Zahir* to *al-Batin*.

But Aquinas incurred an even larger debt to Ibn Rushd when he gave up the Church-sanctioned method of paraphrase, in explicating the meaning of a text. By adopting Ibn Rushd's hermeneutics, he introduced a technique of close and deep readings of original texts in the preparation of his commentaries. Here, too, we see the sleight of hand by which Christian ideologues could, in a single gesture, honour Ibn Rushd as 'The Commentator' and diminish him in importance as a mere transmitter of ideas rather than an original and creative intellect. There are 503 explicit citations of, or references to, Ibn Rushd in Aquinas' collected writings: the thought of the Angelic Doctor could not have been conceived without the thought of the Cordoban master (Fletcher 1993: 134).

The intellectual face-off between the Averroists and the Church marked the beginning of an Enlightenment before the Enlightenment, a crucial and defining phase in Europe's cultural history. This combat between a theology convinced of its absolute claim to truth yet fearful of rival perspectives, and a philosophy that drew strength from healthy scepticism and critical openness, was decisive to the emergence of modernity. It released the mediaeval mind into the realm of the secular: the realm of rational thought, scientific method, liberal discourse. The guiding spirit of this transformation, Ibn Rushd, was praised and banned depending on the degree of openness of the authorities at various European seats of learning during the 12th and 13th centuries, but eventually, his works became standard textbooks in West European universities, remaining so until the 16th century. As the scholar Miguel Cruz Hernández writes: 'Ibn Rushd was doubly present in the Renaissance: negatively, insofar as the Averroists of the 15th to early 17th centuries were the most rigid scholastics, and positively insofar as his ideas about a strictly rational philosophy and a theology based on scriptures were typical ideas of the Renaissance and the Reformation respectively' (Hernández, in Jayyusi 1994, 797)

Ibn Rushd remained a powerful force in the Renaissance, influencing a gallery of brilliant figures like Pico della Mirandola (1463–1494). Pico was one of the chief architects of Renaissance humanism: philosopher and Neoplatonist, precocious intellectual and Papal protonotary at the age of 10. Friend of Lorenzo de' Medici and Savonarola, he had studied Arabic and alchemy, imbibed Ibn Rushd through a Jewish Averroist tutor, been eulogised for his ideas as well as censured for heresy, all this before he died at 29, possibly poisoned by an enemy. Pico believed that God had created man, not as a part of the chain of Being, but as a sentient being whose purpose was to appreciate God's Creation. This is how he opens his *Oration On the Dignity of Man*: 'Most esteemed Fathers, I have read in the ancient writings of the Arabians that Abdallah the Saracen on being asked what, on this stage, so to say, of the world, seemed to him most evocative of wonder, replied that there was nothing to be seen more marvellous than man' (translated by A. Robert Caponigri). Following Ibn Rushd, Pico taught that when man uses his consciousness to philosophise, he rises towards the angels; and when he fails to exercise his intellect, he vegetates. In terms that recall the intellectuals of al-Andalus, Pico wrote that the exercise of the intellect alone could assure human dignity, for only human beings have the free will to change themselves and their circumstances, rather than being puppets of natural contingency. In his schema, the highest rank is thus accorded to those who employ their intellect and imagination to encompass the totality of Creation: to scholars, writers and image-makers. And so, under Pico's tutelage—and through him, the tutelage of the Arab Aristotelian *falasifa*—the mediaeval artisan grew wings and explored the empyrean, ascending to the stature of the 'genius'. Some Renaissance humanists did not hesitate to acknowledge the debt they owed Ibn Rushd. Look closely at Raphael's 1510 masterpiece, 'The School of Athens', and you will find him there, the only Arab among the Italian artists and intellectuals masqued as Ancient Greek philosophers.

❧

Ibn Rushd was not the only teacher from Mediterranea whom Aquinas learned from and then put behind him. He admitted that his response to the central question of *Utrum necessarium sit homini habere fidem* ('Whether it is necessary that man have faith?') was an exact copy of a response made before him by another Cordoban thinker, and Ibn Rushd's contemporary: Musa ibn Maimun al-Qurtubi. Known to posterity as Maimonides (1135–1204), he was born into the intellectual elite of Cordoba like Ibn Rushd. While Ibn Rushd's father and grandfather had been *qadis*, Maimonides' father was a rabbi. Like all cultivated Jews in al-Andalus, he spoke and wrote in Arabic, for which reason—improbable as it may seem in a period of bitter polarisation between Israel and the Arab world—the masterpiece of Judaic thought that he composed, *Dalalat al-Hayirin* (*A Guide to the Perplexed*), is written in Arabic. He left his home country and settled down at the court of Sultan Salah ad-Din al-Ayyubi in Cairo (the Saladin of Crusader lore, the Kurdish Mameluke ruler and Defender of Islam who frustrated repeated attempts by the knights of Europe to conquer Palestine), becoming the Sultan's court physician. Amazingly, despite holding such a sensitive state position, Maimonides was permitted to write and publish his arguments against Islam's official view of Judaism and Christianity as 'falsifications', as traditions that had betrayed the divine revelation of the Word of God. In some Islamic countries today, certainly in Saudi Arabia and Pakistan, he would have been threatened with execution for blasphemy. Even more importantly, he was allowed to codify Jewish religious law in the *Mishne Torah*, which he wrote in Hebrew: it became one of the foundational texts of Judaism. So not only was classical Hebrew literature a child of Arabic literary models, as we have seen from the work of Samuel ha-Nagid, but the cornerstone of Judaic theology was written in Arabic and thus naturally inspired by Islamic thought!

But Ibn Rushd and Maimonides—these two legendary Cordoba-born philosophers and intellectual leaders whose influence would ripple far beyond al-Andalus, into Christian Europe and further, into global modernity—had the misfortune of living though the period when, for the first time in the history of al-Andalus, the Party of Faith had prevailed over the Party of Reason. Both died far away from the beloved city of their birth, Ibn Rushd in Marrakesh and Maimonides in Cairo. In such times of persecution, Maimonides, a master of camouflage, advocated a dissembled conversion as a way out for suffering Jews; Ibn Rushd, for his part, practised the philosopher's courage in the face of adversity.

For, despite his celebrity in Christian Europe and his long-term impact on the course of modernity, Ibn Rushd was not a hero at home. Ironically, while his contribution to Christian and modern Western thought is incalculable and of foundational value, he left virtually no mark on Islamic thought. His exile, towards the end of his life—although it was subsequently rescinded and he was permitted to rejoin the Almohad court—marked a symbolic end to the liberal and progressive aspect of al-Andalus. Together, Ibn Rushd and Maimonides symbolised the last flowering of a tradition that had begun in the Baghdad of Harun al-Rashid in the 8th century and had in many ways reached its zenith at this inhospitable moment.

It could be argued, not unreasonably, that the Islamic world condemned itself to bigotry when it rejected one of its greatest thinkers, Ibn Rushd, and the entire lineage of *falasifa* that he embodied. Instead, Islam turned to the now-unchallenged zealots of the Party of Faith.

೧೪೮

The great achievement of the Arab thinkers was not to return the Aristotelian cat to Christian Europe, plump and content after centuries of pampering in sunnier climes, but to present them with a roaring desert lion they had never known. Before that, Christian Europe had recalled the names of Plato, Aristotle and Plotinus with a veneration that was in equal parts nostalgia and ignorance. The *falasifa* shocked intellectuals in Christian Europe into an awareness of how the Ancient Greeks could be re-examined in the light of current experience, how their ideas of healthily skeptical self-discrimination and informed, independent judgement could be used to constructive effect. The *falasifa*, far from being couriers delivering precious messages from classical antiquity to the Renaissance, were guides who—by personal example, erudite commentary, polemic and teaching—paved the way for critical inquiry, the empirical temper, and the primacy of individual reason over the totalitarian claims of ecclesiastical authority. Indeed, they paved the way for that separation of Church and State, and the liberal and secular public sphere that we take for granted today, cherishing it as a triumph of the Enlightenment. Al-Kindi, al-Razi, Ibn Sina and Ibn Rushd prefigured Montesquieu, Diderot, Rousseau and Voltaire. The East/West boundary breaks down in philosophy as well: the *faylasuf* was the ancestor of the *philosophe*. A conclusion that the 12th-century scholar Hugo of Santalla would have had no trouble with. Sitting in a library in Aragon, he recorded a sentence of counsel for his fellow Latinists: 'It befits us to imitate the Arabs especially, for they are as it were our teachers and precursors in this art' (Burnett, in Jayussi 1994, 1051). When we celebrate the foundation of modern secular society, we should not be praising the 'Christian tradition', as we often do, but the great tradition of confluence.

The Siamese Twins

At first glance, the piazza seems to be in Venice. It even resembles the Piazza San Marco. But as we enter the vast painting, the signs that point towards the East multiply. There are minarets and obelisks in the background, as well as camels and giraffes, and many of the notables assembled in the foreground wear Oriental clothes: the men in turbans and fez, the women in *hijab*. We recognise Turks, Persians, Ethiopians and even some Tartars among them. The title of the painting affirms this impression: 'Saint Mark Preaching in Alexandria'. This masterpiece by the brothers Gentile and Giovanni Bellini (commissioned in 1492!) epitomises the relationship of Venice to the East. For the architecture in this painting is neither there nor here; it is a visionary design that expresses the fascination, or even love affair, that Venice had with its twin across the sea, Alexandria. The church in the middle of the canvas is a basilica reminiscent of Hagia Sophia, with a contemporary Venetian façade. Its domes are unmistakeably borrowed from Mameluke royal tombs. Some of the houses are adorned with Egyptian grilles and tiles; the famous *kelims* hang from the windows. In other words, the urban landscape of this painting merges Venice with Alexandria. For the patron saint of Venice, St Mark, was the founder of the Christian Church in Alexandria and was martyred there in 75 CE. And the fact that he stands gloriously at a pulpit, expatiating to a congregation of Italians and Orientals, speaks of the self-assurance of resourceful Venice. Gentile and Giovanni Bellini, the leading Venetian painters of the time, constructed a Siamese twin of a city, in which legendary origin and modern desire are woven together into a gesture of pride. A pride made possible by the daring act of merchants from Venice who stole the relics of St Mark from Alexandria in 828 CE. According to the legend, the enterprising Venetians had covered the relics with slices of pork—anathema to the Muslim *douaniers* checking their goods. By that time, Venetian ships had begun to make regular journeys into the Muslim part of the Mediterranean. Initially, the laws of Venice had forbidden trade with Alexandria and the territories conquered by the 'Saracens', but after the relics had been won back, the insecurity expressed in this regulation fell away. In the year 971 CE, the trade in wood, metal and weapons on the market of Alexandria was explicitly permitted. Venice maintained friendly relations with Egypt for centuries, unaffected by the Crusades, by the downfall of the Fatimids in the 12th century, and by the *coup d'etat* of the Mamelukes. This exposure to the Eastern bazaars transformed Venice itself, in the art historian Giuseppe Fiocco's phrase, into a 'colossal *souk*'.

Bellini's painting shows how seamlessly the currents of West and East flowed into one another in those days. The concept of absolute dichotomy arose much later, and we need to stretch our imagination to get a feel of this fluidity.

Pepper! The currency of neighbourly exchange, so costly that victors levied tribute from those they defeated in pepper. *Pippali!* A pungent spice from south-western India that cheated the taste buds to accept meat that had gone bad. *Filfil!* A small black pod so potent that it gave Venice mercantile strength and enhanced its curiosity about the East. Shipped to Venice from the Malabar coast through Jeddah, Alexandria and Damascus, it was exported to Vienna, Nuremberg, Paris and elsewhere in Central and West Europe. As usual, location was the key to fortune: for centuries, Venice was the hand that reached up towards the Alps and beyond from the long, richly embroidered sleeve of the Adriatic.

That hand would offer muslin and velvet, pearls and lapis lazuli, silk and perfumes, saffron and cinnamon, glass and tiling, porcelain and tapestries: all the signs of eastern luxury and opulence that animate European paintings during the Renaissance and the Baroque (indeed, the word 'Baroque' is itself derived from the Arabic *burga*, meaning uneven, rocky ground, absorbed into Portuguese as *barocca*, meaning a large, irregularly shaped pearl).

The Bellinis' responsiveness to the cultures (and opportunities) of the Orient was not an exception, but the rule: many Italian artists were experimenting with eastern themes and settings, and seeking commissions from eastern patrons. In 1479, the Doge of Venice 'loaned' Gentile Bellini to the Ottoman Sultan, Mehmed II 'the Conqueror', the principal result of which was the magnificent Bellini portrait of the emperor, now in the collection of the National Gallery in London. Two years later, Costanzo da Ferrara was commissioned to design a bronze portrait medal of Mehmed, which he rendered as an appropriately equestrian imperial image.

Da Ferrara visited Istanbul several times between 1470 and 1480. The time he spent on the East/West divan yielded a series of drawings and paintings inspired by the Ottoman and Safavid art that he saw. One of these, a gouache and pen drawing, 'Seated Scribe', is a wonderful portrait, at once sensitive to the sitter and stylised. Some years later, like a letter sent to an unknown recipient, 'Seated Scribe' was answered by a Safavid or Ottoman painter of distinction, most likely Bihzad of Herat. He has rendered a variation on da Ferrara's image in gouache and goldleaf, attending to his subtly detailed Renaissance realism, its discreet shadows imparting the figure volume through the folds of a turban, the bunching of a sleeve or the contour of facial features in changing light. But he prefers to translate these to suit his own preference for a figure removed from time, set against a flat field, lit up with an inner radiance, the pattern on its robe almost alive. It is as though the Safavid or Ottoman painter were working, in and through da Ferrara, towards an imaginary lost original from which the Italian took his cue—a search that does not reproduce tradition, but generates innovation. 'Each artist draws on the aesthetic innovations of the other, making it impossible to say which painting is definably "western" or "eastern"' (Brotton 2002, 137–38).

The Florentines were not far behind the Venetians. In 1504, Leonardo da Vinci, in his role as military engineer, offered to build a 350-metre arched bridge across the Bosphorus for Sultan Beyazid II. This fantasy never found practical expression; the Sultan then opened negotiations with Michelangelo, which proved equally futile. It may shock many readers, brought up on the understanding that 'East is East and West is West', to learn that the finest artists of Renaissance Europe were participating in such a flourishing cultural exchange with the 'infidel' in the decades following the fall of Constantinople in 1453, a triumph of Mehmed's military acumen. A gift for ignoring borders and an interweave of cultural amplitude, commercial enterprise and scientific curiosity distinguished Europe's leading minds in the late 15th and early 16th centuries: as unblinkered research in the geniza of the Renaissance now reveals, artists of the stature of da Vinci, Michelangelo and the Bellinis clearly saw themselves as denizens of Mediterranea, and welcomed the opportunity to execute commissions of portraiture, surveying or engineering for the Ottomans and the Mamelukes (both Muslim powers were rivals in commerce, incidentally), just as they did for the electors, doges, merchant-princes and condottiere-dukes of Christian Europe (Jardine and Brotton 2000).

⚮

From the last decades of the 15th century onwards, Venice became one of the world's printing capitals. Hundreds of publications poured out of its presses, catalysing the sciences in Europe and eventually opening up a liberal sphere sustained by the diffusion and availability of knowledge formerly confined to courts and monasteries, and with it, the possibility that any citizen could hold, articulate and publish his opinions. In 1494, Luca Pacioli's *Everything about Arithmetic, Geometry and Proportion* provided readers with the first comprehensive introduction to these subjects, including a guide to double-entry bookkeeping. In 1531, Otto Brunfels edited a medical compendium of the writings of Serapion the Younger (Ibn Sarabiyun, 9th century CE), which defined the modern science of botany. In 1537, Niccolo Tartaglia benchmarked the existing state of knowledge in physics in *New Science*. In 1545, Geronimo Cardano published his *Great Art*, the first algebra primer.

Among the books published in Venice during this first great wave of printing was Aristotle's *Works*. This gorgeous 1483 production speaks of confluence on several levels: not only does it document the original text as well as the commentary by Averroes (Ibn Rushd), but the elaborate illumination that surrounds the text shows the two masters holding converse in a pastoral landscape populated by frolicking satyrs. On another level, the new technology of moveable type co-habited with the visual appeal of the hand-painted illuminated manuscript, with its elaborate rubrics. This, one of the most sumptuously produced printed books to emerge from Venice, is a testimony to the beauty of the hybrid.

Through the printed word and, as importantly, the printed image, readers in Europe learned, not only of the philosophers of the Islamic world, but also of inventors, astronomers, surgeons and pharmacologists. Readers in Florence and Padua learned of al-Jazari (1136–1206 CE), whose work in automation provided inspiration for some of da Vinci's mechanical inventions. Al-Jazari wrote *The Book of Knowledge of Ingenious Mechanical Devices*, engineered ingenious contraptions and anticipated cybernetics. He built divertimenti-like water clocks featuring a mechanical circus of zodiacal signs or planetary systems; a toy orchestra of performing musicians; a fountain in the shape of a peacock, with mechanical slave figures dispensing soap and towels—but also complex hydraulic systems equipped with pumps, wheels, scoops and gear systems, and the first segmental gears.

But perhaps most impressive of all is the influence that an all-but-forgotten Perso-Arab astronomer named Nasir ad-Din at-Tusi (1201–1274 CE) exerted posthumously. Director of the Caliphal observatory at Maragha in Persia, at-Tusi had corrected Ptolemy's time-honoured account of the motion of the spheres. His theorem of the 'Tusi couple', which demonstrates that 'linear motion can be derived from uniform circular motion', was central to Copernicus' work of three centuries later: 'Historians of astronomy have now realised that Copernicus reproduced the Tusi couple in his *Revolutions*, and that the theorem was crucial in defining his heliocentric vision of the universe. Nobody looked for Arabic influence upon Copernicus and his European contemporaries, because the assumption was that there was nothing to find... this example suggests that even more discoveries await scholars prepared to investigate the vigorous but now neglected exchange of ideas that took place between east and west' (Brotton: 199).

A Healthy Balance

Part of this book was written in Mainz, in an apartment on the top floor of the Johannes Gutenberg Museum. It was a beautiful experience to be reminded of an epochal invention that all of us take for granted, as we take the most essential inventions for granted. They become so much a part of our lives that it never enters our minds to conceive what the world would have been like without them. Take numbers away, for instance, and we collapse at a single stroke. We very nearly did in 1999, when the world awaited the advent of the new millennium with the same holy dread that had afflicted people a thousand years previously, when the Apocalypse was believed to be at hand. And why? Because of a veritably Cabbalah-like formula: Y2K, the merest whisper of which threatened to drive all our computers crazy. Banks wouldn't be able to access our accounts for us. Supermarkets wouldn't be able to sell us our bread and wine, with the bar codes failing. Navigation would die on pilots, planes would fall from the sky. Phones wouldn't work, doors wouldn't open to frantic bell-ringing. Wealth and poverty would be made equal. Suddenly, and for many of us it was a sensation we hadn't felt since school, we learned to respect zeroes and the rest of the infinite procession of numbers again, dancing in and out of our lives like ghosts.

Mainly zero, though. Or *sifr*, in its Arabic form, from which we get our 'cypher' and 'decipher'. The Arabs themselves correctly called their numbers 'Hindu numerals', since they had adapted the concept of a decimal place value system, its calculations based on a set of nine numerals and a null quantity, from Indian mathematicians and astronomers like Aryabhatta, Bhaskara and Varahamihira. By 760 CE, Arab scholars had embraced this system, whose efficacy ranged across a variety of computations, from the simplest household accounting to the most intricate navigational or astronomical positioning. Without Hindu-Arabic numerals, we would all have turned into the kind of contortionists among whom Dante pictured Michael Scotus the magician. In this Inferno of Innumeracy, we might have spent our lives trying to multiply MDCCLVIII by CDLXVI.

Christian Europe may well have had to use calculators as big as cathedrals, had it not benefited from the efforts of four men widely separated in time and place, and the chance encounters that brought their efforts together: a French monk who studied in the Umayyad Caliphate of Cordoba, was suspected at home of sorcery, and ended his span on earth as pope; a Persian mathematician who had corresponded with colleagues further east, and was about to develop an unheard-of art of balance; a hard-pressed English monk who translated him from the Arabic into Latin in

Toledo, and was interrupted at the task by what he regarded as the bizarre request for a translation of the Koran; and a Pisan merchant, brought up in North Africa, who was Arab in style and speech yet Latin in intellectual expression.

Gerbert of Aurillac (c. 945–1003) was a gifted mathematician, inventor and ecclesiastical politician. As a novitiate, he had been sent to study in the monastic environs of Vich, 60 kilometres north of Barcelona, and the abbey of Santa Maria de Ripoll. He gravitated to al-Andalus, to the universities of Cordoba and Seville, and some whispered that he might even have studied at the Islamic university of al-Kairouan in Fes. A keen student of Arabic astronomy, he wrote a book on the astrolabe, and another on the abacus, and introduced both instruments into Christian Europe. He also built a hydraulic organ, far ahead of the times in its construction. He had mastered the Hindu-Arabic system and could do complex calculations in his head. But none of this was well received, nor did his knowledge pass into common usage. In 10th-century Northern Europe, to which he returned after his student years in the emirates of Mediterranea, there were no vast volumes of trade requiring quick and efficient calculations. There was no popular demand either for literacy or numeracy, no receptiveness to new ideas beyond the small community of thinkers and enthusiasts in which the Christian monk-scholar lived. Both friendships and enmities were often epistolary, carrying over the distances between one secluded monastery and another. Like many Christians who had studied in the Islamic world, Gerbert was regarded by his critics as a wizard in league with the Devil. Their anxieties were not assuaged even after he was elevated to the papacy as Sylvester II, the first

Frenchman to wear that august mitre. The Hindu-Arabic numerals would have to wait for a more propitious time in Europe (Goody 2004, 58).

Like most of his contemporaries at the Bait ul-Hikma, al-Khwarizmi (who died in 850 CE, a century before Gerbert was born) was a one-man orchestra and its conductor too: he was an astronomer, a geographer, a mathematician, and an eloquent writer of Arabic prose. Comparing Indian models with earlier Babylonian solutions, he codified a simple and practical numeral system that anyone could use. Algebra was his brainchild: he pioneered the method of *al-jabr*, which denotes transposition, as a way of restoring equilibrium by adding or subtracting the same quantity on both sides of an equation threatened by instability. He demonstrated the principle of the square root, recognised that equations could be used to describe complex relationships, and noted the role of unknown factors by using a symbol like 'x'. He thus 'opened the door wide to the advanced mathematical procedures that became possible in later centuries' (Turner 1997, 48). The systematic step-by-step procedure that he developed to solve problems is universally used and literally bears a version of its inventor's name. Although 'Algorithmi' looks nothing like 'al-Khwarizmi' on paper, that was the closest his Latin translator could get to the difficult pronunciation: *Algorithmi de numero Indorum*, or 'Al-Khwarizmi Concerning the Hindu Art of Reckoning'. It was a prolonged effort for Robert of Ketton, who had interrupted this labour to undertake the first Latin translation of the Koran in Toledo. Maybe that explains the faults of his Koran-translation. After all, as this votary of scientific knowledge had explained to Peter of Cluny, he needed to conserve his energy for the daunting task of introducing Europe to a completely new branch of mathematics (Menocal 2002, 179–82).

Gerbert's unfinished project was realised in 1202 CE by a merchant called Leonardo Fibonacci (1170–1250), an Arabised Pisan who grew up in the Maghrib, and is today better known for the number sequence named after him. Every number in it, except the first two, is the sum of the two preceding ones, all the way to infinity (1, 1, 2, 3, 5, 8, 13, 21…). The sequence is manifested in many natural contexts—the branching of trees, the spiralling of shells, the arrangement of pine cones—and Fibonacci's speculations on it would have been informed, through Arab sources, by the work of Sanskrit grammarians researching quantitative prosody, who called it *matra-meru*, the 'great mountain of metre' (in modern times, Bartók used it as the conceptual frame for his 'Music for Strings, Percussion and Celesta'). But at the dawn of the 13th century, Fibonacci had more on his mind than shells, pine cones and poetic metres. He triggered off a revolution with his book, *Liber abbaci*, in which he argued convincingly for the introduction of Hindu-Arabic numerals—which he called the *modus Indorum*, the 'Indian method'—and explained the advantage of using them for accounting. The North was now the 'fast-developing world' and the adoption of modern mathematical and banking skills had become necessary, if its merchants were going to transact efficiently with their shrewd and experienced counterparts from the Arab lands, from Persia, India and Ethiopia. In Fibonacci, we find an example of confluence informed by pragmatic necessity: his proposal for the use of Hindu-Arabic numerals in accounting, and the alacrity with which it was taken up, closely resembles the manner in which the Ancient Greeks adapted the alphabet from the Phoenicians. In each case, Europa had to catch up with changed circumstances in Mediterranea—if Europa did not learn quickly, through apprenticeship, collaboration and even complicity with the Other, it would be very difficult to stay in the game, much less get ahead of it.

The importance of maritime trade as a prerequisite for confluence cannot be emphasised enough. Fibonacci's methods were first adopted in the mercantile nerve centres of Venice, Florence and Genoa, as a new language of engagement with the growing complexity and institutionalisation of commercial activity. Accounting on the double-entry model also emerged during this period: improvised by the Arabs in Mediterranea, it had already been practised for several generations by 1494, when Luca Pacioli put it into print in *Everything about Arithmetic....* It is an enduring product of the mercantile complicities between the Adriatic and Egypt, the Ottomans and the Venetians, that ran parallel to, sometimes subverting and at other times ignoring the religious wars between Christianity and Islam. Many of the banking innovations of the Renaissance were outcomes of Europe's apprenticeship to the Arab world, as a word like 'cheque' attests: it comes from the Arabic *sakk*. Paper money and indeed, even today's increasingly plastic money, originates in the promissory notes that were widely honoured (and had to be, if the agent wished to retain the trust of his peers) as symbolic of the vast volumes of money involved in the transcontinental trade in pepper, salt, spices and textiles that linked depots in western India, through entrepots on the Red Sea coast and the Levant, to their destinations in the

Adriatic and Central Europe. Signs for the actual payments—too heavy to haul around the world in sacks—they were sustained by an intermeshing of profitable relations that would make a default suicidal. The institution of the bank itself came into being around this grand trade that ran across East/West lines: many of Europe's leading families owed their fortunes to it. The importance of this new level of efficiency acquired from the East cannot be underestimated, when we think of the role played by mercantile and banking dynasties like the Medici of Florence, and the Fuggers and the Welsers of Augsburg, in underwriting the cultural blossoming of the Renaissance. By the 16th century, these families presided over the earliest multinational corporations (not counting the Church, of course), with business interests in banking, spices, silver, gold and much else spread across India, Africa and the Americas.

Perhaps the Fibonacci sequence is not so irrelevant to the process of intercultural learning, after all: it demonstrates, with all the abstract refinement and compelling precision of a mathematical model, that any process of growth aiming for infinity gathers strength from summations that have gone before.

Conflict and Confluence

The crusade had been going on for quite a while. The non-believers had been attacked in their villages, smoked out from their towns; they had been killed in battle or massacred after surrender. Mercy was not part of the arsenal. God's viceroy on earth, a Pope who had chosen the fitting name of Innocent III (1198–1216), had called for the extermination of the heretics, who were slandered with all manner of perversities. The victims called themselves 'pure believers'; they professed to live in accordance with the teachings of the One sent by God, they were eager to set up a paradise on earth. Towards the end of the crusade, one of the largest towns of the heretics had been besieged in vain for months. The order came through to set the whole town on fire, including the Church of the Madeleine, in which 7,000 women and children had taken refuge. But some of the men in command protested. 'What of all the innocent, good Christians in town, will they suffer too?' they asked. 'Kill them all,' the papal legate exclaimed, 'and the Lord will find his own.' On 22 July 1209, some 20,000 inhabitants were burned to death, and the town of Béziers was plundered and destroyed.

The First Crusade was a brutally successful enterprise— most of all in the South of France. And its primary targets were not Saracens or Moors, but Cathars and Albigensians, communities of radical anarchistic Christians, who had defied the authority of the Vatican. Just 25 years after the siege and burning of Béziers, the fortress of Montségur was conquered and, once again, its defenders were massacred to the last man, woman and child. The heretics were not only thoroughly defeated, they were exterminated. The First Crusade marked the first large-scale, cold-bloodedly planned and well-organised genocide in human history.

Until this point, the conflicts that raged throughout the Mediterranean, though they had been serious, often bloody and brutal, had not been informed by an annihilatory impulse. Once the fighting was over, cultural relations were resumed. Al-Andalus is perhaps the best example. During the eight centuries of its existence, it lived through innumerable local skirmishes and regional wars. But rarely did these conflicts escalate into the negation of the Other. With the exception of the intolerant regime of the Almoravids (first half of the 12th century), the rulers in al-Andalus safeguarded the rights of all its inhabitants, whether Christians, Muslims or Jews. The treatment of minorities is not only the touchstone for the tolerance of a society but also a measure of confluence.

In 1009, a civil war broke out in al-Andalus, leading to the fragmentation of the previously unitary Muslim polity into *taifa*s or independent fiefdoms or principalities. In 1031, when the Cordoban Caliphate expired and the period of *fitna* or strife began, factionalism led to a cultural explosion. The result seems like a paradox, but only on paper: when borders shift and citizens find themselves in a new political environment literally overnight, their cultural activity flourishes. Some borders are impermeable only in hindsight.

Above all, and this is the major difference to the destruction of Béziers, the rulers themselves would not have regarded their battles as annihilatory. As Alfonso the Wise testified: 'The most honourable action of my rule was that I founded together with the Muslim philosopher Mohammed el-Rikuti a school in Murcia where Christians, Jews and Muslims taught side by side.' Great moments of cultural innovation are sustained by political fragmentation—revolutionary cultural edifices are built on political quicksands. Small fiefdoms, fiercely independent, in perpetual conflict with one another: the world of the Greek polis, the Andalusian *taifa* and the Italian *civita*.

Conflict and confluence coexist, sometimes within individuals, who develop ways of dealing with the paradox of inspiration within aggression. Fighting against another religion or an antagonistic polity is a major way of interacting with an alien culture. There often existed a mutual attraction between opponents, as the example of the Knights Templar shows; they became close to Islam while they were fighting the 'Saracens' as Crusaders and settled down in the Levant, profiting from their banking contacts in the Arab world, before they too were destroyed by the Catholic Church as heretics.

Many Christian intellectuals in the era of the Crusades approached al-Andalus with wonderment, even if they judged it from the high horse of religious supremacy. But there was always a handy excuse as to why they as Christians had much to learn from the abhorrent Muslims. The most bizarre of which must have been the sophistry concocted by Daniel of Morley, one of the Latin translators working in Toledo. Towards the end of the 12th century, he proclaimed that the 'New Israel', meaning Christendom, should seize the treasures of Pharoah, in the spirit of Moses. This is the major difference from the perceptions of today. However strong the animosity might have been, in those days Islam was regarded as a role model, with the richest libraries on earth, the most advanced technology and a highly attractive sophistication.

From the very beginnings of al-Andalus right up to its dramatic end in March 1492, conflict between Christian and Muslim polities was the order of the day. After the Arabs and Berbers crossed the Straits of Gibraltar in 711 CE, they occupied the whole of Iberia within a decade. And from the very beginning, the battle lines were not as clearly drawn as one might think. One explanation for the swift

progress the Muslim forces made, was the fact that they
were welcomed by the local population: always by the Jews,
who had suffered great persecution, and sometimes even by
the Christians, who were glad to get rid of their despotic
rulers. And the famous Battle of Poitiers in 732 CE was far
less important than the myth that it gave rise to. Myths are
great simplifications—in reality, conflicts often open up new
spaces of complex interaction. The Berber leader Munnuz
(or Musura), for example, settled down in Cerdagne in the
eastern Pyrenees, married a daughter of Oddon of Aquitaine
and lived as a Muslim duke before he was defeated in 729
CE by the emir of Cordoba, against whom he had rebelled.
Or, the *patricius* Maurontius, who opened the gates of the
city of Avignon to the Muslims in 734 CE (Cardini 2000,
21, 22). Later in the history of al-Andalus, we come upon
El Cid: in legend a stout defender of Catholic Spain, in
reality a soldier-of-fortune who served both Christian and
Muslim rulers, and when setting his sights on the Emirate
of Valencia, allied himself with both sides depending on
expediency. Affiliations crossed the lines of simple allegiance
to one's religion or heritage. The individual's interests were
best served by a free and undogmatic choice of allies.

Similarly, the justifications for alliances were very
adaptable. Probably few people today will remember the
Turko-Frankish tradition, but for centuries, the Western
hatred for Constantinople found articulation in a coalition
with the Arabs, underwritten by an inventive mythology:
'The anonymous Norman knight who was in the entourage
of the Prince of Taranto during the First Crusade, wrote in
the *Gesta Francorum* about the warlike qualities of the Turks
and then came to the legend, according to which the Turks

and the Franks were both descendants of the Trojans and were therefore natural enemies of the cowardly and dishonest Greeks. This is the first reference to a literary topos that was later to be used to justify the opposition to the Byzantine Empire—a topos that has been used repeatedly from the Middle Ages to modern times' (Cardini 2000, 114).

The hagiographies, on the other hand, beatify fanatics, as was the case with the celebrated Mozarab (Arabised Christian) martyrs, about 50 Christians, who supposedly resisted conversion by force and bravely suffered a horrendous death in 855 CE in Cordoba. In fact, these self-obsessed religious maniacs were as alienated from society as the terrorists of today: men and women of extreme action, who were intent on martyrdom. When initially faced with a lenient reaction to their provocations, they had to exacerbate their abuse of the prophet Mohammed until the judges had no option but to order them beheaded. The limits of religious tolerance were well-known to everyone, as is made clear even by a partisan Christian author like the Saxon nun Hroswitha: 'The Muslim rulers issued a pronouncement that whoever so desired to serve the eternal King and desired to honour the custom of his sires, might do so without fear of any retribution. Only a single condition he set to be observed, namely that no dweller of the aforesaid city should presume to blaspheme the golden idol's name (i.e. the Prophet Mohammed) whom this prince adored' (Menocal 2002, 70). The so-called Mozarab martyrs staged their death as a political statement, playing the heroic victim.

Victimhood features high among the prevailing stereotypes of life under Islam in the popular imagination, from Western Europe through the Balkans all the way to

India. It is generally claimed by the ideologues of conflict that churches and temples were destroyed on a grand scale and that the faithful were forced into conversion or ended up on the stake. Without downplaying the iconoclastic and intolerant tendencies within Islam, it should be pointed out that the destruction of churches and the oppression of non-believers were exceptions and not the rule. This holds true of India, Al-Andalus, the Levant, the Balkans and many other territories that have come within the fold of Islam. In India, the list of destroyed temples in the eight centuries of Islamic rule amounts to less than a page and certainly does not extend to the key pilgrimage sites of Hinduism, some of which were patronised by Muslim rulers (for example in Varanasi, Braj, Dwarka, Puri, and Srirangapatnam).

The myth of forced conversion is possibly the most emotive tool of ideological falsification. At the onset, the conquerors of Iberia constituted not more than one per cent of the population. The conversion of the population was a gradual process that lasted centuries so that it was only in the later period of Al-Andalus that the Muslim population was the majority. After 500 years of Muslim rule, there was still a substantial Christian population in the Emirates of Iberia; on the other hand, today, after 500 years of Christian rule, the only Muslims to be found in Spain are illegal workers from the Maghrib.

Muslim authorities had little interest in mass conversion. Omar, who conquered Iran towards the end of the 7th century, issued the command that the Persians were *not* to be converted because the taxes they were paying as non-believers financed the occupying force. Throughout its first hundred years, Islam in Iran was, in the words of

Karen Armstrong, 'a garrison religion'. Similarly, the Vizier in Istanbul wrote to the local government in Ottoman Bulgaria to put an end to the alarmingly rapid voluntary conversion of Christians. The Bulgarians were converting for tax-evasion purposes; the Vizier wanted them to remain Christian for reasons of state finance. Such is the double-entry bookkeeping of conversion.

The standard mythology, untainted by such nuances, constructs a horror scenario of victims being spiritually enslaved and alienated from their true tradition. In this black-and-white portrait, there are only the resolutely unconverted and the forcibly converted. But even enthusiastic converts, notorious for their strict and dogmatic understanding of their new faith, cannot help carrying with them elements of the cultural landscape they came from—as the example of Petrus Alfonsi has shown. Completely missing from the picture is, however, a third group: the inhabitants of the in-between.

In cosmopolitan cities like Alexandria, Baghdad, Toledo or Palermo, the cream of society chose to incorporate different traditions into their life. Identities are mostly portrayed as static and innate phenomena, and people of multiple origin or plural life choices are usually suspected of potential schizophrenia. 'How do you combine two souls in one breast?', such people are asked. 'How can you live without a fixed *Heimat*?' The answer is more than simple: most individuals are plural selves, extending themselves through apprenticeship and camouflage, shifting identities tactically, or as the social context or their personal vision demands, adapting to the fault lines of existing conflicts, but not subservient to them.

This is why the idea of a Clash of Cultures is nonsensical. Culture is that part of human experience and expression which cannot be co-opted into the banality of polar confrontation.

III

The Gifts of the Magi

NATIVITY PLAYS

The original story is deceptively simple, its facts as bare as the desert landscape in which it unfolds. Several wise men of eastern provenance follow a star over the western horizon until they reach a village where a newborn baby lies asleep in a manger. They honour the child, prostrating themselves before it, and present the parents with gifts before departing homewards. This is about all we know of a scene that was embellished in later times, the men given different ethnic identities and legendary names, their arrival re-enacted in Nativity plays. So powerfully did this simple story kindle the imagination of generations to come that, today, whether in the Lutheran or in the Orthodox Church, in Latin America as well as in India, the wise men are commemorated in one of the most central feasts of the Christian sacred calendar. In Germany, this festive occasion, which falls on 6 January, is known as Heilige Dreikönige, the 'Three Holy Kings'; elsewhere, simply as the Festival of Epiphany, a word that means, in Greek, 'to shine upon, to reveal, to manifest'. The symbolic relevance is evident: the wise men acknowledge the universal message of Christ, foreigners as they are to the land of Judaea. But, although Caspar, Melchior and Balthazar have been depicted in innumerable paintings, on mosaics and church windows, although one of them was made out to be an African, the second an Arab or Persian, and the third a European, and although their gifts of gold, myrrh and frankincense became synonymous with the riches of the Orient, their true identity and the implications of their presence in the Nativity story have usually been misread. In the original text of the Gospel of Matthew (2.1–12), they are described as *magoi*, the plural of *magos* (in Latin, *magus*), a word derived from, and denoting, the Magian priests of Iran. Scholars have pointed out that this word was used in the wider sense of 'wise man' in the time of Matthew; but the fact that the Evangelist did not employ the far more common and inclusive word *sophistai*, and that they are defined as men from the east, supports the assumption that they truly were Iranian priests. For the little we are told of the wise men's behaviour points to an origin in the Iranian cultural sphere, just across the eastern border of the Roman Empire (the popular song has the wise men 'travelling afar', but their homes were not all that distant from Judaea). By addressing the infant Messiah as 'the King of the Jews', they reveal their belief in the concept of divine kingship, a concept that was developed, as we will show, in Persia. According to this concept, the divine king had to be legitimised by the consecration of the priests, and the precious, symbolic gifts mark this ceremony of legitimation. This ceremonial 'king-making' was a central role of the Magian priesthood in imperial Persia. Even the complete prostration that the wise men offer (Matthew writes that they 'fell down and worshipped' Jesus) is historically accurate, for that is how the Persian priests worshipped. There is also an adequate explanation for the wandering star, which, to sceptically minded readers, has always seemed rather esoteric: to the Magian priests, who were trained astrologers, the stars were guiding angels.

Of course, this story, which is recounted only by the Evangelist Matthew, plays a greater role in folklore than in theology. But it directs us towards some of the defining sources of the cult of the new Messiah. For without the extraordinary creativity of Iranian religion, not only Christianity, but also the other Abrahamic religions, would not have taken the form that they did. Many of us were brought up on a cultural diet of Heaven and Hell, God and the Devil, the Saviour and the Day of Judgement, winged angels and haloes. The sheer familiarity of these visions might explain our belief that they are inherently 'ours'. But, in fact, these conceptions were acquired from Iranian tradition by the Jews taken into captivity in Babylon during the 6th century BCE.

Iranian religion encompassed a wide spectrum of beliefs, most of them bundled under the rubric of Zoroastrianism— the message of the prophet Zarathushtra. Today, at a distance of about 3,000 years, it is difficult to discern which of the revolutionary concepts coming out of Iran can be attributed to Zarathushtra, or to the worship of Mithras or to the cult of Zurvan. What we know for certain is that, by the 6th century BCE, certain beliefs were well established, which were not only new to the history of ideas, but which would also formatively influence Judaism, Christianity and Islam.

Although usually, and inexplicably, left out of the enumeration of the world's monotheistic religions, Zoroastrianism was one of the earliest monotheisms. Zarathushtra preached the message of the Supreme Lord, Ahura Mazda, the sole force of creation that maintains the cosmic order. The Hebrews were previously not monotheists, neither in the understanding of the Zoroastrians nor in our contemporary sense. Typically of a tribal religion, they merely argued that they were the chosen people of their particular god. In Genesis, the term 'elohim' is used, but it actually means 'gods'. For obvious reasons this is translated as God in modern times. The American scholar Morton Smith has pointed out that the Hebrews were divided amongst those who worshipped Yahweh next to other deities and those whom he calls 'the YHWH-Alone Party' (Elias, for example, means 'my God is Yahweh', which only makes sense, if there are several gods on offer).

Zoroastrianism developed the principle of duality: the contest between good and evil, the fundamental antagonism between the equally matched God and the Devil (in Zoroastrianism, Ahura Mazda in the corner of light and Angra Mainyu in the dark corner). In order to establish the supremacy of God over the Devil, this antagonism cannot be conceived of as an endless battle staged across eternity; if redemption is to be gained, then time must have an end.

Evil is a constantly present force, which might lose out momentarily, in small skirmishes, to the Good; but its existence is never threatened. Therefore, the supremacy of the Good can only be established conclusively through an apocalyptic climax, a final battle between God and the Devil, which ends with the triumph of Good and the death of time. We know this solution as Armageddon, followed by the Day of Judgement.

But before this curtain call can be taken, an intermediary figure had to be introduced, who offers the human being a chance of redemption and announces the end of time— the all-too-familiar figure of the Saviour, in Persian the *Saoshyant*. It is the Saoshyant who leads the forces of Good during the final battle, and establishes the Timeless Time that follows the End of the World. Zarathushtra calls this heaven '*Feresho-kereti*', translated as 'The Making Wonderful'. In the words of the hymn called the *Zamyad Yasht*, humankind will find the guarantee of salvation, and

> '... *from that day on will never grow old and*
> *never die,*
> *will never decay and never be corrupted,*
> *ever living and ever increasing, and master*
> *of its wish;*
> *when the dead will rise,*
> *when life and immortality will come,*
> *and the world will be restored.*'

Compassionate redeemer and warrior-judge, the Saoshyant stands at the head of a tradition called soteriology, one of the most influential concepts ever to have been disseminated into global religious thought. As we will see, this concept entered Buddhism. In Mahayana Buddhist thought, the Saoshyant became Maitreya, the Buddha of a future cycle, and an elaborate philosophy and ritual developed around him and similar saviour figures, whose worship to this day defines the 'Pure Land Buddhism' of East Asia. Entering Hinduism, the Saoshyant metamorphosed into Kalki, the Promised One, the tenth and last avatar of the god Vishnu.

Above all, the Saoshyant directly inspired the Messiah of Judaism and eventually imparted his aura to the newborn in the manger of Bethlehem: by the 2nd century CE, the Saoshyant had become the Christos of Christianity, the Anointed One. Since then, there has been a periodic explosion of saviour cults throughout the world, some of them inspiring vast popular movements, others lapsing into charlatanry, or worse, misleading their votaries into mass suicide. Centuries after the ministry of Jesus, the concept of the Promised One percolated into Islam: in the Shi'a and Ismaili versions of that religion, he is the Mahdi or the Hidden Imam, who will reveal himself in his glory and mercy on the Day of Judgement. It is surely no coincidence that the Shi'a population is chiefly concentrated in what was once the dominion of Zoroastrianism—Iran.

The Saoshyant is assisted, in his mission, by the *yazatas* or *amesha-spentas*, the star-angels or Immortal Spirits produced from the thought-energy of Ahura Mazda. These guardians of virtue are the originals of the archangels of Judaism, Christianity, and Islam: intercessors between Heaven and earth, bearers of revelation. In the iconography of Iranian religion, a particular mark of blessed distinction attended these star-angels: their heads were circled by the *khvarena* or aureole of glory. The *khvarena* became a global mark of divine status: the halo around the heads of the Bodhisattvas in Buddhism, the Tirthankaras in Jainism, the high deities Vishnu, Shiva, Ganesha and the Devi in Hinduism, and of Christ, the Virgin Mary and the saints in Christianity. So when Christians celebrate Epiphany, and the arrival of the Three Wise Men from the East, they are unwittingly commemorating the philosophical, spiritual and aesthetic gifts of the religion of the Magi, gifts far more valuable than precious metals and spices.

THE BLESSINGS OF CAPTIVITY

600 years before the Magi travelled westward to Judaea to pay reverence to the newborn King, the people of that country were driven eastward into captivity in the land of the Magi. The destruction of the Temple of Jerusalem and the deportation of the Hebrews in 587 BCE by the Babylonian monarch Nebuchadnezzar ranks high among the catastrophes experienced by this nation. It was certainly endured as a traumatic loss; nevertheless, only a few generations later, Judaism would rise like a phoenix from these ashes. At first, displacement and loss of sovereignty translated into religious disorientation for the Hebrews. Their nation had been annihilated, the foundations of their religious self-identity had broken down: Yahweh, their tribal god, had failed. Not only had he not protected his chosen people, but his primacy was eclipsed by the gods who presided over the imperial splendour of Babylon and later, of Persia (Cyrus the Persian conquered Babylon in 539 BCE, establishing a unified empire). In a close reading of the Old Testament books referring to this period, the American scholar Jack Miles convincingly shows how the god of the Hebrews was perceived to have withdrawn into inactivity. Re-formatting him as a unique and omnipotent deity, as we will see, was one reaction; the other was to glorify the human drama of the Jewish nation, expressed most radically in the Book of Esther, a narrative set at the Persian imperial court, in which God is not present at all.

Like individual exiles, a people in exile always compares between the tradition it carries, and the new world in which it finds itself: strengths and weaknesses are noted and internalised, until part of one's tradition is no longer seen as cultural wealth, but rather, as excess baggage, which is replaced by the superior aspects of the new environment. The intensity of the acculturation depends, of course, on the openness of the host society and its political and cultural paradigms. In Babylon, these inclined towards further liberality and acceptance when Cyrus came to power. He did not 'single out the Jews alone, but accorded the same freedom of departure and worship to all the exiles of Babylon. And he showed equal liberality to those who stayed, recording his magnanimity on a cylinder of baked clay which once called out to the nations, but was found, millennia later, under the tumbled ruins of the city, and today sits mutely in a glass case in the British Museum' (Kriwaczek 2003, 182).

In what way was the Iranian religion a model to a defeated and broken people? To begin with, it was anchored in a codified revelation: the *Gathas*. Zarathushtra called himself *manthram*, one who is able to compose mantras, or verses of power. 'Just as the Holy Spirit descends like a dove into Jesus immediately after his baptism, so Zoroaster's original vision occurs after he emerges from a river ritually purified to be led by a shining being into the presence of his God' (Roberts 1995, 156). The power of the word was enshrined in the culture that the exiles were exposed to. In a process that started sometime in the second half of the 6th century, Hebrew scribes and legal experts resident in Babylon started putting together the Torah. This sacred text would become the axis of religious activity, its portability and reliability a replacement for the lost localities of worship symbolised by the destroyed Temple of Jerusalem. In the absence of a sacred space of ritual, the exiles congregated to read the holy texts, thus finding refuge within scrolls of parchment rather than beneath a roof of cedar. Although the Temple in Jerusalem would be rebuilt, less than a century after the deportation, the Torah would in future stand at the centre of prayer and ritual.

With the death of the tribal Yahweh, God appeared on a more elevated, universal plane. Back home, the prophet Jeremiah had reason to lament that the Hebrews were worshipping other tribal gods, and straying from Yahweh ('Surely, as a faithless wife leaves her husband, so have you been faithless to me, O house of Israel, says the LORD.' Jeremiah 3. 20) This is just one of a barrage of jealous accusations and expressions of insecurity. What a difference to the omnipotent God of Isaiah ('I am the Lord and there is no other, besides me there is no God'), who is heroically invoked just a few decades later. Isaiah had been deported to Babylon in 587 BCE, and the book of prophecy named for him, like those of Daniel, Nehemiah and Ezekiel, was composed in exile. The power and the glory of Yahweh are the dominant themes of these prophetic songs. As if the glorifications of the Iranian texts were being cited, with the names of God being substituted.

In the apocalyptic visions of Isaiah, Ezekiel, and Daniel, it is the universal Supreme Lord, the 'Most High God', who is invoked in all his sublime, even overwhelming and terrifying grandeur—clearly the God-image of Iran. These visionary books evince an imagery of radiant, monumental, winged presences that arrive on clouds, blazing with metal, surrounded by the aura of unceasing fire; they are heralded by the sound of rushing waters or winds, and they speak in voices of thunder. What sounds like hallucination, was part of the everyday-life in Babylon: monumental icons of the Babylonian royal deities Marduk and Ishtar, answering to this description were housed in vast temple-palace complexes like the *ziggurat* and taken in procession.

With the dramatic opening stanzas of Ezekiel's prophetic visions, we are plunged into the baroque sacred imagery of Zoroastrianism. One of the earliest deportees from Judaea to Babylon in 598 BCE (his visions probably date to 593–571 BCE), Ezekiel speaks of a flaming wheel (the symbol of Ahura Mazda!), of four-winged guardian angels *(the fravashis)*, of griffins as well as of four-winged creatures, each bearing the heads of a man, a lion, an ox and an eagle. All these seemingly bizarre creatures were common Zoroastrian representations, to be seen in the ruins of Ecbatana, Susa and Persepolis, or in the British Museum. How amazing to realise that these winged symbols also stand for the Evangelists: the man for Matthew, the lion for Mark, the ox for Luke and the eagle for John! So Ezekiel has completely incorporated a foreign imagery into a vision for the future of his own religious nation.

The most drastic and memorable adaptation occurs in the Book of Daniel, a Jew who rose to high office at the court of the monarch Nebuchadnezzar. Appointed chief of the Magi of Babylon, he was respected above all the other magicians, enchanters and astrologers, for his visionary powers and integrity, and accorded the exalted Old Akkadian title of 'Belteshezzar' ('May He Protect the Life of the King'). The Book of Daniel is one of the most extraordinary documents in the Bible: its sacred visions introduce a cluster of new ideas that would be central to the Perso-Hebraic religious reinvention soon to be codified as Judaism! The pivotal points of the narrative are the visions vouchsafed to Daniel by the 'Most High God': 'I saw in the night visions, and behold, with the clouds of heaven there came one like a son of man, and he came to the Ancient of Days and was presented before him. And to him was given dominion and glory and kingdom, that all peoples, nations, and languages should serve him; his dominion is an ever-lasting dominion, which shall not pass away, and his kingdom one that shall not be destroyed' (Daniel, 7, 13–14). The son of man, of course, is now familiar to us as a title of Jesus, his advent derived from the Persian Saoshyant, his regal power from the concept of divine kingship, a means of legitimising the absolute power of the monarch, who was seen to partake in the glory of the Supreme Lord. The Saviour, riding on 'the clouds of heaven', announcing the End of Time, demarcates the horizon of Hebrew Messianic expectancy.

The entire book of Daniel bears testimony to the revolution that took place in Babylon, and offers proof of how captivity turned into captivation. Angels as we today conceive of them (the *malochim* of the Genesis were merely 'messengers') are first described here: as winged beings, possessed of unimaginable powers of speed and given names. The seven post-exilic angels (Gabriel, Michael, Raphael, Israfil, Israel, Uhiel and Uriel) are clearly modelled on the seven *Amesha Spenta* ('immortal spirits') of the Avesta.

For the first time in the history of Hebrew thought we read in Daniel of the promise of resurrection after death for some and retribution for others. Until the Babylonian captivity, the Hebrews had neither fleshed out their idea of the afterlife nor had they put it into ethical perspective. Sheol, the underworld, was no more than a place of darkness that awaited the dead regardless of how they had lived their lives. Zarathushtra had conceived of both the bodily resurrection of the dead as well as the Last Judgement that awaited them to determine whether they would be condemned to eternal torment or enter paradise (the word 'paradise' begins to appear in Jewish literature at this time, from where it is inherited by the early Christians. It is derived from the Persian *peri-daeza*, the enclosed garden of the angels). 'Prior to the exile there had been among the Hebrew peoples no real interest in the afterlife, which was seemingly discussed only in the vaguest terms. In fact pre-exilic Judaism was distinctly non-eschatological. (...) The Jews ... progressively adopted the Zoroastrian belief in the matter of eschatology, for the ideas of reward and punishment following death begin to appear in Hebrew literature from this period, and, later still, the concept of complete separation of good from the evil—familiar from the Zoroastrian *Gathas*—is one that figures prominently in some Christian texts concerning eschatology' (Clark 1999, 153–54). It was up to Daniel to trumpet a warning as well as a call to hope, the coming of judgement and resurrection, of reward or punishment (Daniel 12, 2).

☞☜

The Hebrews who were resettled in several waves included the political and intellectual elite, taken as hostages, a widespread practice of imperial warfare at the time. Once in Babylon they certainly did not all become hewers of wood and drawers of water. Intellectually agile, many adapted to local culture, until Persian became 'to a great extent the language of everyday life among the Jews of Babylonia' (http://jewishencyclopedia.com/articles/8951–judaeo-persian). They had become adept at negotiating with the system, seizing the opportunities that it offered while tackling the perils of envy or conspiracy that talented exiles have always faced from entrenched local elites. A number of Jews were employed as secretaries, scribes, astrologers, court bureaucrats, and legal experts. Even their names changed: Esther is the undying mother goddess Ishtar, while Mordechai, a key figure in the Book of Esther, is named for the jubilant cry uttered after the annual sacrifice and revivification of the god-king, '*Marduk khai!*' (Marduk lives!).

The connection between the Mesopotamian-Iranian religious complex of Babylon and the Hebrew religion is intimately organic. It was modulated by men whose instrument was the word, whose ability to read, write, orate and engage in divination gave them power among their own people as well as in their adopted society, and allowed them to make critical comparisons between their scriptures and those of their hosts—to modify, assimilate, adapt and import new ideas. The Torah, the Jewish Law, codified in Babylon, was probably brought to Judaea from Babylon by the priest and scribe Ezra, who bore gifts from the Emperor Artaxerxes to the Temple of Jerusalem. Ezra played a complex interreligious and intercultural role. He was Artaxerxes' personal choice for governor in Jerusalem, explicitly ordered by the emperor 'to make inquiries about Judah and Jerusalem according to the law of your God, which is in your hand …' (Ezra 7, 14). Ezra was given sweeping executive powers: 'Whatever Ezra (...) requires of you, be it done with all diligence...' (Ezra 7, 21–23). Evidently, Ezra is regarded as a trustworthy member of the Persian elite, someone who would pacify and civilise the Judaean people according to the political exigencies of the Empire. He would operate through the instrument of the recently codified Torah, which Artaxerxes seemed to regard with considerable respect, a clear sign that its ethics were not too far from his own *Weltanschauung*. Ezra was not the only such 'Persianised' prophet of emerging Judaism. His contemporary Nehemiah, earlier the cupbearer of Artaxerxes, also served as governor of Jerusalem. Both prophets, returning from exile as cosmopolitans with a clear sense of superiority, defined the authoritative canon of Judaism, claiming precedence over those who had remained behind. It might seem a paradox that the result of far-ranging hybridisation was proclaimed as the true faith, while the natives left behind in the backwaters were forced to adapt. 'Thus I cleansed them from everything foreign', Nehemiah exults (13, 30). The new had evidently become the authentic. Or, as Stephen S. Wise, Chief Rabbi of the USA, once wrote: 'The return from Babylon, and the adoption of the Babylonian Talmud, marks the end of Hebrewism, and the beginning of Judaism.'

THE ETERNAL CONSTRUCTION SITE

God might be a woman to some, but His son was certainly no blond, and the early evolution of Christianity indisputably took place outside Europe. The pivotal Councils of Seleucia, Nicaea, Alexandria and Chalcedon were all held in the East. Most of the clerics who attended these high-power conferences of the early Church came from Asia and Africa: from the lands that are today Turkey, Syria, Iran, Egypt, Tunisia, Libya and Algeria. The new religion received its name, 'Christianity', in Antioch, where St Peter had established his bishopric. And during its first millennium, many of the cultural innovations of the new faith emerged from the Eastern Church, for the Second Rome was far more sophisticated than the old Rome.   CRAFTWORK METAPHOR

Religion is not an edifice built in perfect accord with an omniscient architect's blueprint, but a work in progress. It involves an army of designers, engineers, builders, masons and residents, each with his or her own aspiration. They cooperate and compromise with each other; but they can also fall out and fight bitterly over the look of the façade, the decoration of the interiors, and the layout. This contrasts with the dogmatic model of religion promoted at Bible schools, medersas, yeshivas, gurukuls and *viharas*, and disseminated from there into the popular understanding. As a result, although the remembrance of God is a constant feature of religious practice, the many names and forms by which He/She was invoked along the way are carefully forgotten. Father Hugo Rahner's position, chosen at random, typifies this position: 'Christianity is a thing that is wholly *sui generis*. It is something unique and not a derivative from any cult or other human institution, nor has its essential character been changed or touched by any such influence' (cited in Finley 1977, 171).

Historical memory is an unwelcome guest at the banquet of belief, even in secular societies. And where religion reigns supreme, it runs the risk of being denounced as blasphemy, reason's defiant attempt at questioning revelation's claim to uniqueness. Every organised religion regards itself as a monumental temple, constructed from homogenous elements. But when we walk around inside it, we find domes floating unmoored above arcades, columns detaching themselves from plinths, and doors hinging open to spirit us away into catacombs painted with incongruous frescoes. Many of these elements date back to before the advent of the prophet or teacher who founded the temple; some have nothing in common with his stated vision. The common term for this dynamic process is 'syncretism', which is normally used to describe a deviance from orthodoxy and an attempt to taint a religion's unique character by admixture with other belief systems. But in truth, if syncretism is defined as 'the attempt to combine or reconcile different beliefs or practices', then all religions are inherently and continuously syncretistic.

๑๛๑

When Christ assured his followers that 'in my Father's house are many mansions', he might have been describing the Levant, which was, at the beginning of the Current Era, a bazaar of competing cults, a laboratory for spiritual experimentation. Among the Jews themselves, there was no zealously codified Judaism from which heretics could be accused of having strayed. At the top of the Jewish pyramid stood the Temple aristocracy, the Pharisees and Sadducees familiar to us from Biblical stories. But the Talmudic rabbis record that the imagination of the Jewish laity was claimed by at least 24 different schismatic groups informed by Weltanschauungs as diverse as asceticism, hedonism and Platonism. Among these were the Hasidim, the Herodians, the Therapeutae, the Boethusians, the Sicarii, the Hellenes and the Zealots (Kriwaczek 2003, 165–66). And this was just the situation within the Jewish orchard—Monty Python's depiction of rival groups in 'The Life of Brian', who differ only in their acronyms is as historically grounded as it is hysterically funny. Beyond it grew trees of luxuriant and variegated foliage, grafted and cross-bred to result in a forest of hybridity: the Egyptian cults of Isis, Orisis, Cybele and Serapis, in their late-Roman forms, had built up a mass following. The region was home, already, to Adonis, the Syrian fertility god; and the Iranian solar god Mitra, having been assimilated as Mithras, the Slayer of the Bull, had attracted the legions of Rome to his standard.

And beyond this forest lay the desert and the mountains, where communities of hermits had retreated into caves, to spend their days in prayer and contemplation, awaiting the turning of the wheel that would overthrow the corruption of the cities and reinstate purity of soul. Among these figures were preachers like John the Baptist, who had committed themselves to a Messianic vision and raised their voices in the wilderness, believing that the End of Days was at hand and the people must be prepared for the Lord's advent. Some of these recluses were demonstrably influenced by the teachings of the Buddha, which had been transported to the Levant from India and Central Asia along the Silk Route that connected Kashgar (in today's Sinjiang) to Antioch. The Essenes who composed the Dead Sea Scrolls—their 'Teacher of Righteousness' strongly suggestive of the Teacher of Dharma from further east— were active in the spiritual counterculture that was turning away from the Judaic political elite, whose Hellenisation and Romanisation had alienated them from the common people. This diversity of patterns was to be integrated, whether acknowledged or not, into the architecture of Christianity.

∞

Religions that are still in the process of forming themselves develop a voracious appetite for symbol and doctrine, no matter what kind of tables these are laid out on. At the Last Supper, Jesus distributes pieces of bread and passes a chalice of wine among his followers, telling them that by this token—by eating his flesh and drinking his blood—they shall participate in his mystery and be assured of everlasting life in the hereafter. The sacrament of the Eucharist, so central to Christianity, has its origins in the earliest religions of fertility, in which the young king-god had to be sacrificed in spring, dismembered and eaten, in order to ensure the harvest and the well-being of the community. Adonis, the Syrian god, comes to mind at once. His temple was called the 'House of Corn': in Hebrew, *Baith la-Haim*, ergo Bethlehem ... it appears that the blood and flesh of the Christ mythos is infused with the presence of many previous deities.

Christ shares his birthday—for which the Gospels give no date—with one of these divine predecessors. Mithras, revered by the Roman army and several Roman emperors who rose from the military, as *Deus Sol Invictus*, the 'Unconquered Sun God', was said to have been born on the winter solstice, when the days begin to grow longer again: in the Julian calendar, this day fell on 25 December. The emperor Aurelian (270–274 CE) declared it a holiday throughout the Roman Empire. Late in the 4th century, as the influence of Mithraism began to wane, its adherents were drawn into the Christian fold, and the high point of its ritual calendar was absorbed into the cultus of the rising Son of God as Christmas.

All the ancient religions enshrined the Great Mother, the principle of fecundity who presided over the earth: she was worshipped under many names, as Ishtar and Innana in Mesopotamia, Isis in Egypt, Nanaia in Inner Asia, Devi in India, and as Demeter and Maia in Greece. When Greek colonialists in Asia Minor found temples to her, they named her Artemis and took over the existing cult: from this encounter would rise one of the seven wonders of the ancient Mediterranean, the temple of 'Diana of the Ephesians'. Christianity's new recruits would have wished for some place for this approachable figure of compassion in their new faith, which was dominated by male figures—and not surprisingly, it was at the Council of Ephesus in 431 CE that the cult of Jesus' mother, the Virgin Mary, received official sanction, and permission was granted to paint and sculpt icons depicting her with the Infant Jesus. This Council legitimised the use of the title *Theotokos* for Mary: the Mother of God, who would intercede with her son on behalf of distressed humankind (Russell 1994, 26f). The goddesses of antiquity continued their steady ascent into the new Christian system, as aspects of the sainted Virgin Mary. During the reign of Julian the Apostate, the pagan goddess of victory, Nike/Victoria, was successfully absorbed into the adoration of Mary—who is also known, in some contexts, as Maria Victoria, 'Our Lady of Victories'.

Perhaps we should speak of Christianities rather than Christianity, during the early centuries of the Current Era, before an unambiguous body of dogma—pronounced by an ecclesiastical authority backed by imperial power—was imposed on the various regional interpretations of the Word of Jesus and the Myth of Christ. In the shifting borderland between a multiform Judaism and these rival Christianities, many sects arose and conceived bizarre doctrines. Had any of these secured the imagination and military power of an emperor, we might have grown up with a very different Christianity. The mysterious Elchasaites, for instance, believed that a revelation had been made in the year 100 CE to their founder, Elchasai or Elchasaios ('The Lord's Secret Power'), by two gigantic angels. These celestial messengers— one male, the Son of God, and the other female, the Holy Spirit; both 20 miles high—told Elchasai that Christ would be reincarnated century after century, each time being born of a virgin. They also instructed him to venerate water as the source of life, and passed on a mystic formula to be used by his followers in the event they were bitten by a mad dog or a snake (Dalrymple 1997, 66–67).

Elchasai was a chef who delighted in flavouring his revelation with an assortment of doctrinal masalas. His followers observed the ancient Jewish Mosaic laws, circumcising their male children and scrupulously keeping the Sabbath. But Elchasai declared the Jewish use of fire for sacrifice to be an error, and also rebuked the Zoroastrians for venerating it as a symbol of the Divine. Being of the water persuasion, he claimed to have received the certain knowledge from his angels that fire was abhorrent to God. The Elchasaites were baptised by water, and sworn

to practise vegetarianism and celibacy. Elchasai banned
joy and laughter from his spiritual dominion; he forbade
his followers all intoxicants, as well as music, painting and
other arts. Preoccupied with ritual cleanliness and hatred
for the infernal world in which they found themselves,
they occupied themselves with tilling the fields around
their settlements close to the head of the Persian Gulf, near
present-day Basra. They loved Christ, but hated St Paul,
'the Apostle to the Gentiles', and refused to recognise the
authority of his systematic account of Christian belief and
his Epistles as an addition to the New Testament (Kriwaczek
2003, 98).

৩৯৬

Jewish-born intellectuals like Paul, formerly Saul of Tarsus
(c. 10–c. 67 CE), and Philo Judaeus, also called Philo of
Alexandria (c. 25 BCE–c. 50 CE), had been raised and
educated in a manner that was more Helleno-Roman than
Judaic. They were proud to be citizens of the Roman Empire,
spoke Latin and read Greek in preference over Hebrew,
wrote in these classical languages, and were arguably more
attuned to the philosophical teachings of Plato than to
the prophets of the Old Testament. Many of the Helleno-
Romanised Jews also adopted the customs of their pagan
neighbours, and often assimilated themselves so completely
to the Roman provinces of their residence that they were
scarcely identifiable as Jews. Many took on Helleno-Roman
names; some sought surgical means of undoing their ritual
circumcision, so as to appear even physically more like the
Gentiles (Paul alludes to this practice in I Corinthians 7:18).
At times, even their worship was influenced by their pagan

surroundings: archaeologists have discovered an ancient synagogue at a site called Dura-Europos on the Euphrates River, where scenes from pagan mythology are depicted in the mosaics and the paintings on the walls.

When some of these Helleno-Romanised Jews joined the Christian movement, they took their classical training and taste with them, marking a crucial shift from the Aramaic-speaking peasants, fishermen and artisans who had formed Jesus' original circle. What followed was a vigorous interplay between early Christianity and Greek mythology, philosophy and religion. Gradually, under the influence of philosophers like Philo, the ethical cast of early Christianity yielded before a more mystical interpretation based on the exalted nature of divine utterance: the Word, the Logos of Greek philosophy transported into a Hebraic context, came to stand for the wisdom of God, which mediates his absolute and ineffable nature for the benefit of his creation, by implanting itself in human intelligence and suffusing itself through nature. As Werner Jaeger wrote in *Early Christianity and Greek Paideia*, 'Among the factors that determined the final form of the Christian tradition, Greek civilisation exercised a profound influence on the Christian mind' (quoted in Finley 1977, 170).

Philo remained steadfastly Jewish throughout his life, dedicating himself to interpreting the Pentateuch and defending Judaism against Gentile critics by situating it in its historical, philosophical, ethical and juridical contexts. But his teachings, arising from his need to resolve the central contradiction of his life, were to influence Christian and Muslim, mystical and rationalist thinkers for 17 centuries. For Philo was an embodiment of intellectual crisis: he was the first Jewish thinker to taste the freedom of Platonism, and the first Platonist to chafe under the regulations of Judaism. As a Jew, he was bound by the scriptures of his fathers, revealed to them by a God absolute in His omnipotence and thus demanding of obedience. But as a Platonist, he was free to exercise his intellect, regardless of the pagan gods who were in any case merely symbolic figures, with the ideal of perfection residing in a realm of ideas that was free of a specific religious context. Standing at the cusp between opposed traditions, Philo became the first philosopher to ask how speculative thought could be reconciled with Biblical revelation, whether in metaphysics or epistemology, ethics or physics. In the process, Philo worked his way towards a doctrine of monotheistic mysticism, teaching that the human mind is capable, by intuition rather than by reasoning, of apprehending God's existence but not His nature. As we have seen in the sub-chapter 'The Faith Party vs. the Reason Party', this tension between reason and revelation, as well as science and mysticism, was to preoccupy the Arab Aristotelians of Mediterranea, the Averroists of Europe, and virtually every major European thinker all the way through the Renaissance and Reformation to the Enlightenment.

Classical philosophy died in the 6th century CE at the hands of Byzantine Christian state terror, as we have seen in the sub-chapter 'Alpu Betu Gamu'. But there was a happy period in the early centuries CE, when the Christian soul was wide open to intellectual stimulation, and pagan philosophers took substantial possession of it. In the 2nd century CE, Clement of Alexandria devoted a great deal of scholarly attention to discovering Christian implications in Greek myths. To men like Clement, the new faith could only achieve intellectual respectability if it could be woven into the sophisticated tapestry of Helleno-Roman thought. It could scarcely make much headway among the Roman Empire's elite as a religion of subaltern resistance fashioned to serve the oppressed of provincial Judaea. Clement virtually claimed many of the Greek masters, both mythical and historical, as Christians *avant la lettre*. He refers to Orpheus as 'the theologian', and speaks of Plato as being 'under the inspiration of God'. Even the Epicurean Metrodorus is praised for having uttered certain words that were 'divinely inspired'. Clement's writings disclose the breadth of his knowledge of classical as well as Biblical literature. His treatises are heavy with copious citations; according to the tabulations of scholars like Stählin, Clement cites some 359 classical and other non-Christian writers, 70 Biblical writings (including Old Testament apocrypha), and 36 Patristic and New Testament Apocryphal writings (including those of heretics). The total number of citations in his collected works is 8,000, more than a third of these culled from pagan writers. Of Greek-inspired Christian teachers like Clement, who became the founders of Christian philosophy, Werner Jaeger writes: 'They led their pupils to that spirituality which was the common link of all higher religion in late antiquity. They began to remember that it had been Plato who made the world of the soul visible for the first time to the inner eye of man, and they realised how radically that discovery had changed human life ... On their way upward, Plato became the guide who turned their eyes from material and sensual reality to the immaterial world in which the nobler-minded of the human race were to make their home' (Jaeger 1963, 137).

Several centuries would pass before Christianity achieved

the critical mass—the right mix of imperial support, popular following, ecclesiastical authority and codified dogma—to present itself as a free-standing monument, the 'thing *sui generis*' of Father Hugo Rahner's fantasies, and deny most or all of the drafts, versions and models that had gone into its building. By the time religions reach this stage of grand canonisation, they have given up the mobility of imagination for the stasis of consolidation. At this stage, the religion establishes its distinctive identity through the gesture of difference. It marks off its own special revelation by seeking to refute or denounce others. Veiling adaptation with amnesia, it declares its own doctrines, rituals and observances to be unique and primordially revealed—and incomparably superior to all other claimants to religious truth. All similarities are explained away as variation or coincidence, all absorptions stripped of the traces of their origin. The greater the stability achieved by the new system, the more furiously the gifts of confluence are sought to be denied. The crucial gesture of canonisation is to erase the chisel grooves and emery grazes of mixed origin, and to replace them with the bland polish of a foundation mythology.

Travelling Back in Faith

The Vishwa Hindu Parishad (VHP) is a powerful organisation founded on the belief that the Hindu religion is eternal and unvarying, that it has existed in India for thousands of years (the VHP's chronological estimates vary between 8,000 and 50,000 years), and that its essence has never been affected by any foreign influence or borrowing. Hinduism is unique to India, and India is a uniquely Hindu country: such is the logic of the VHP. And yet, occasionally, the VHP is assailed by a sense of doubt. It is all very well to thunder at Muslims and Christians in self-congratulatory public meetings, its leaders say to themselves, but it would be nice to have some proof with which to fight off the scoffing scientists. And so, as documents recently made available to researchers reveal, the high command of the VHP decided to sponsor a time-travel project, sending a fact-finder back to the glorious Vedic age to collect evidence of how the ancestors of the Hindus performed their rituals, worshipped their gods, and conceived of their relationship to the Divine.

Thus a card-carrying member of the VHP, a Hindu of impeccable credentials, embarked on a pilgrimage through time, back to 1500 BCE. He must have been very excited at the prospect of seeing with his own eyes the Golden Age of his belief, when the tenets of Hinduism were still untainted by any alien influence. Landing on the banks of the Indus, he immediately sets out on a walk, eager to visit the temples of the area, to pay his respects to the gods, magnificently carved in stone, and to celebrate the sunset with the time-honoured ritual of the *aarti*. Our contemporary Hindu searches in vain. He encounters some herdsmen, but none of them has heard of his supreme god, Shiva. Vishnu does ring a bell, but only as one of the names of the sun god. He stumbles from one shock to another: the mention of the loving Krishna provokes anger, for Krishna, they tell him, is a cattle-raider, the enemy of their chief god, Indra. And when he asks about Ganesha, most popular of today's deities, they nearly chase him away—that dangerous trouble-maker, they whisper, can only be appeased by tribal shamans from the forest on the far side of the river. Eager to mollify his new friends, the perplexed guest asks about their gods. The ancients rattle off a long list—Varuna, Mitra, Agni, Kubera and others—but to him these are vague names, shadowy figures, either forgotten or demoted, as in the case of Kubera, to goblin status. I will find consolation in a temple, our time-traveller thinks to himself, but the locals do not understand his request. The word '*mandir*' is foreign to them, as is '*murti*'. Where the heck are you from? they ask with growing suspicion. Are you one of us at all? After much to and fro, they lead him to a temporary altar by the river, around which several men are seated. But he can make no sense of their shamanic rituals of purification and praise; he does not know the guardian spirits and fertility goddesses that they are worshipping. In great inner turmoil, he proceeds to a sacrificial clearing in the forest, hoping at least to come across a familiar idol. But alas, there is not a single one there, only strange totems: instead of the mighty Shiva, he encounters a cobra; instead of the regal Vishnu, he finds a fish, a tortoise and a boar. And when the sun begins to set, he is all alone, and the locals give no sign of gathering for the congregational evening prayer that has been his daily spiritual fare for as long as he can remember. But the locals are hospitable, and after dinner (of which the less said the better), they sit around the fire with him, struggling to make conversation. Seeking common ground, he narrates some of his most cherished myths as best as he can in his high-school Sanskrit, the story of Rama and Sita, the saga of the feuding Pandavas and Kauravas, the legend of the rival sisters Ganga and Parvati. His audience is entranced by such beautiful tales from foreign lands, not only because of his story-telling skills, but also because their ears have never been charmed by anything similar to this. Even the most central of Hindu concepts, which he idiomatically mentions in passing—the *karma* of his life—baffles his Vedic 'ancestors'. But there is one comforting moment, when they invite him to a sacrifice: the *yagna*. With enormous relief he casts the mix of sesame, clarified butter and kindling wood into the fire, to the chanting of Vedic verse. But his relief is short-lived. He is scandalised that the priests hand around a brew they call *soma*, and shocked by the readiness with which both women and men drink it, transporting themselves into states of dream. He is eager to return home, for he might as well have landed on the moon.

೧೯೦

But the VHP does not give up so easily. OK, they exclaim, so we exaggerated by a millennium here and a millennium there, but that doesn't prove anything. Our researcher must have missed the great Hindu unravelling by a sliver of time—we just have to send him out again. This second journey falls under a bad omen right from the start. Bereft of hopes and illusions, our Hindu is mortified by the thought of what else he might find in this most alien land of all—history. Travelling ahead in time from where he left off, he labours on desperately. His patience is sorely tested. He has to overcome oceans of strangeness, to hack his way through jungles of disorientation. The forms of worship that he comes upon shock him with their earthiness and their lack of inhibition: the snake and the penis, the gnomes and goblins. Well, he says to himself, the temples must have been made of timber and brick, although he can't quite imagine such constructions living up to the proclaimed greatness of Ancient India. He reaches the 5th century BCE, the epoch of the great religious founders Gautama Buddha and Mahavira, who were born just a few miles apart in North India. The way he has been taught history, Buddhism and Jainism were offshoots of Hinduism, but he has not yet come across a Hinduism he can identify with, except for a few hymns and some rudimentary rituals. Branches without a trunk? He ponders over the puzzle, slipping further into the marsh of confusion when he realises that the very first monuments he stumbles upon—towards the 2nd century BCE—are Buddhist, the domed stupas of Bharhut and Sanchi. So if the Buddhists managed to build such impressive monuments in stone, why not the Hindus of that era?

Soon after this, he comes across a glimmer of hope: a column, six majestic meters of sandstone, standing in Besnagar in Madhya Pradesh. It lacks any figural representation, but the eagle Garuda is perched on its top, a symbol of Vishnu, finally a sign that is known to our traveller. Reading the inscription he learns that the column is the gift of a prominent 'Bhagvat', a worshipper of Vasudeva. *Vasudeva!* That is, Vishnu, a properly Hindu monument at last. Our time-traveller exhales—he is home. Overcome by emotion, he bows down, and his eyes fall on the inscription. For God's sake! The donor is a foreigner: *Heliodoros, son of Dion.* Our man sits down heavily, puts his head in his hands, and tries to understand this cruel blow of *karma*, this reversal of everything he has held holy. Apparently, this ambassador from the Greek kingdoms in the northwest (today's Pakistan and Afghanistan) to the local court is the first documented Vaishnavite in history, the first known person to regard Vishnu as the Supreme God.

Heliodoros' is hardly the exceptional case of an eccentric

convert, as is proven by the coins dug up in the surrounding region. They are minted by Agathokles, an Indo-Greek ruler, and also dedicated to Vasudeva, the very first known image of this deity. Meaning 'the Radiant God', Vasudeva is a new kid on the block, a recent composite welded together from Pan, Dionysos and Indra. But our traveller must traverse another two centuries before he finally encounters a Hindu iconic image of any kind: In Gudimallam, near today's Madras, he stumbles upon a truly magnificent sculpture. One and a half meters high, this icon is widely regarded as the 'earliest depiction of Shiva in Indian art' (Michell 2000, 40). Our traveller is further perplexed: the lingam is not an abstract symbol, but a rather realistic gigantic penis. The deity does not stand independently but steps out of the lingam, at the same time standing on the shoulders of a *yaksha* (a nature spirit), holding a water-pot in his left and an antelope in his right hand, an axe resting on his shoulder. Even more confusing, the figure is devoid of any signs which usually identify this God: the trident in his hand, the river goddess Ganga in his locks, the snakes around his neck, and the bull Nandi behind him—in one word, a depiction sorely at odds with all later depictions. Even the dating (1st century BCE), though widely accepted by scholars, may be open to doubt. It emerges from the connoisseurial mystique of stylistic comparison, particularly imprecise when there is hardly anything to compare it to, conducted by T. A. G. Rao in 1914 (a period when even the datings recognised the prevailing nationalist necessities, and it wouldn't have been patriotic to dispute a century or two). After some reflection, the traveller shakes his head in doubt. Is he really standing in front of Shiva?

Only when he reaches the Kushan period, in the 1st century CE, does the time-travelling Hindu breathe a sigh of relief. In Gandhara he comes across an idol he can immediately accept as Shiva: he carries a trident and rides on the bull Nandi. In Mathura, he finds a sandstone sculpture of Vishnu; and in both Kushan centres he recognises Skanda, the war-god and son of Shiva, a popular divinity among the Indo-Greeks. In the icon of Govardhana-dhara—the young god bearing the mountain—he recognises his own Krishna at last! But for the most part, the images show Buddhas and Bodhisattvas, many of them with faces like *firangis*. He wonders if there is some malfunction in his time machine. Where has the rest of Hinduism gone? Is this really India, or has he been sent somewhere else by mistake, to some kind of Buddhistan? He wants to check with the VHP control centre, but the communication device has failed.

In a Kushan royal shrine, for the first time, he sees the now-popular icon of the goddess Durga locked in combat with a demon. Why do I see the Devi for the first time on my journey? he asks the Kushan custodian of the shrine. Well, says the custodian, I don't know what you mean, you look and sound like a foreigner; but if you really want to know, this is our war-goddess Nanaia. We brought her with us from Inner Asia, and now the locals are very happy with her. They bring her flowers; they sacrifice goats on her big feast day. We don't discourage it. And although we would prefer her to be shown killing a bull, the local artists have been experimenting with a buffalo. And we say, why not, after all it is closer to their experience in this monsoon country, so let them sculpt her killing a buffalo-demon.

Our present-day Hindu spends the rest of the day in

a daze. He avoids entering the other shrines he sees, not knowing what further surprises lie in store for him. But never mind, he tells himself, he is the first living Hindu to have gone back to the past and seen what it was really like. He can make a career out of his stories. He relaxes a little at the prospect.

When he finally makes it back to contemporary India, he presents his findings with great excitement to the VHP's high command. He is promptly expelled from the organisation and his papers are publicly burned. Not for telling things that are untrue—the VHP leadership can hardly assert this claim against his testimony—but because he has dared to state, openly, facts that cannot be tailored to suit the myth-machine. You do not have to be historically correct to be condemned as a traitor, but in today's India, large parts of which are dominated by the ideology of Hindutva, it certainly helps.

A Body for the Buddha

Once, the Buddha was a colossus, his face masked in gold and studded with dazzling gems. But history has obliterated him—no trace remains of the gold and the jewels; no trace remains even of the Buddha himself, only the vast and empty niche that he used to occupy. Today Bamiyan, once a bustling sarai on the Silk Road, is a desolate valley in Afghanistan, a symbol for the apocalypse of intolerance.

When the Taliban blew up the two statues of the Buddha in Bamiyan, in the spring of 2001, the world was outraged by this act of cultural annihilation. However, these icons were more than just the largest statues of the Buddha in the world, they were also the last remaining symbols of a grand but almost forgotten civilisation: the Kushan Empire. Flourishing between the 1st and the 4th centuries CE, this empire drew upon a plurality of sources. The Kushans were the offspring of intermingling between the nomadic Yueh-chi—Turkic migrants from north-western China who spoke an Iranian language—and a local population that already represented a mix of Indic, Greek, Bactrian and Scythian strains. Diversity was a hallmark of this empire, which, at its zenith under the emperor Kanishka, comprised today's Afghanistan, Pakistan, much of northern India as well as parts of Iran and China. It was the first empire in history to straddle the mountains that divide Central Asia and India. Thus, on its eastern margins, this realm interacted with the Indo-Gangetic and Chinese spheres, and on its western margins with Persia and the Graeco-Roman world.

This open society brought about a revolutionary contribution: the representation of the Buddha in human form. Sometime in the 1st century CE, the Buddha achieved iconic appearance for the first time in the history of his worship. To understand the magnitude of this innovation, one has to remember that Buddhism began as an anti-iconic religion, propagated as a message of discipline, emphasising the economy of personal perfection, the practice of compassion and spiritual hygiene. The Enlightened One had expressly forbidden his disciples to remember him through images, and he had been obeyed for seven centuries. Sculptors had conveyed his presence through the blessed footprints, the lotus, the Wisdom Tree, the Pillar of Fire or the empty teaching throne.

What precipitated this transfiguration? The socio-political dynamics of the Kushan Empire had confronted the

Buddhists with new challenges. Successfully proselytising beyond the confines of Indic religious culture for the first time, they were obliged to come to terms with followers of varied religious conditioning. The growing popularity of their message strengthened the hand of those Buddhists who had already been arguing, in the ongoing theoretical debates in the monasteries called *viharas*, that the Buddha should be memorialised in a *charita*, a potted biography of the supreme teacher as an approachable guru. In a parallel process, the new converts translated the abstract symbolism presented to them into the iconic form to which they were accustomed in Persian religion. Additionally, the resplendent sculptures of antique Hellenistic paganism—Apollo and Hermes, Zeus and Poseidon—more secular than sacred, more of the agora than of the temple, served as a role model when the Kushan Buddhists finally decided to cast the Great Teacher in their own image. A style that is now named the 'Gandhara style' after the western centre of the empire. Once the unthinkable became stone, schist to be exact, there was no stopping the sculptors, many of whom were itinerant artists from the Roman Orient, seized by a desire for iconic magnificence. Similarly, the artists in Mathura, the eastern capital steeped in folkloric visuality, now allowed themselves to adapt existing figuration to invent images of the Buddha.

Thus, not only was a new style born, but also a religion re-configured. For the artistic liberties of Gandhara and Mathura are evidence of far more than merely an aesthetic departure. They point towards a wide-ranging rewriting of the original charter of Buddhism, the emergence of what would eventually be called the Mahayana tradition, to which two-thirds of today's Buddhists subscribe. The Bodhisattva is the central figure of Mahayana belief. Literally meaning 'the essence of enlightenment', the Bodhisattva is a seeker who has attained freedom from the cycle of rebirth, but— out of compassion—remains in the world in order to help all beings reach Nirvana. 'The Bodhisattva seeks to become a Buddha because only a Buddha has the knowledge and means to save the maximum number of beings' (Skilton 1994, 110). The accent in early Buddhism was on the individual aspirant, the Arhat, and his salvation through his own efforts. Reaching out to new audiences, Mahayana Buddhism created completely new forms. A closer look at the different Boddhisattvas reveals their affinity with Zoroastrian models: Avalokiteshvara, the friend and protector, has a remarkable closeness to Mithras, the deity Iranians evoked in a direct and personal relationship; Maitreya, who partakes of the name and solar character of Mithras, is evidently modelled after Saoshyant, the Coming Saviour. Most importantly, the Bodhisattvas became the focal presences for a devotionalism that had so far been largely absent in Buddhist practice. Once the sluice gates were opened, all sorts of torrents burst in.

The series of changes transformed the status of the previously rather neglected lay Buddhists. They had derived merit from feeding the monks, who had taught them wisdom stories in return, but beyond this level, Buddhism had been a monastic monopoly. But now, with the concept and the figure of a compassionate guardian at hand, believers could address their worries and wishes directly to the deity. The active participation of householders in the practice gave birth to a meaningful lay Buddhism. Without this development, Buddhism would hardly have been able to spread outside of the monasteries and across Asia. The practical readjustments made in those days by the leading figures of Buddhism are exemplified by the monk-scholar Nagarjuna, best known as the founder of the Madhyamika school, a system of dialectical logic. He successfully carried Buddhism into the deep south of peninsular India, mobilising popular support by importing folkloric deities into the pantheon as subsidiary tutelary figures, rather as the pagan *genii loci* of Europe were adopted into Christianity as saints. His were, so to speak, strategies of packaging and marketing.

The exigencies of devotionalism called for deities that stood for more than the common sacred history. Turning towards the transcendent, the believer extended his attention and expectation into the future, a future in which he would be redeemed personally, and the community would achieve final liberation. A multitude of new Buddhist figures answered this devotional need: Maitreya, Avalokiteshvara, Manjushri, Akshobhya and Kshitigarbha, among many others.

These Future Buddhas are amongst the bewilderingly manifold protagonists of the sacred texts, the extensive *Vaipulya sutras*, all composed or codified in the Kushan era. Lacking canonical authority, these Mahayana sutras were not accepted as such by sections of the Buddhist orthodoxy, but, by articulating the ongoing spiritual explorations, they appealed to the converts. The Future Buddhas were to travel into the Far East through the translator Kumarajiva, forming the basis of the 'Pure Land' versions of Buddhism that are the faith of millions of people today. In defining their novelty the Buddhist historian Andrew Skilton calls them 'visionary dramas', a fitting description for their baroque quality. While early Buddhist texts were terse and to the point, these Mahayana texts stimulate the sensory

imagination, leading the listener through a dialogical form
into lands of mythical splendour, populated by a large cast
of legendary beings. Full of elaborate details, they straddle
the previously perceived gap between the parable and the
epic in Buddhist literature.

But the *Vaipulya sutras* were far more than spiritual
blockbusters. They set the scene for a transformation of
the four ideals of love, compassion, joy and equanimity
from stages of meditation into principles of action. The net
of Indra, the Garland of Buddhas and other concepts of
interconnectedness gained prominence. These radical ideas
mirrored the complex social and political relations during
the Kushan Era. A teaching which claimed that the Buddha
principle was shared by all living beings, that they all partook
of the Buddha-mind, accorded well with an Empire that
sought to encompass many different cultures, languages and
traditions with tolerance and acceptance. The most influential
figures of Kushan Buddhism reflect this reality: Nagarjuna
was an Andhra from Southern India, Vasubandhu came
from Peshawar, An Shihkao was Parthian and Kumarajiva
was the son of a Kashmiri father and a Kuchean (Chinese)
mother. One would be hard-pressed to find another example
of such ethnic and cultural diversity amongst the canonical
figures of any school in any given period.

Naturally, a Buddha with a human body stood in need of
a biography. Until then there had been no full-length account
of the Blessed One's life in canonical literature: 'It is curious
that the canonical writings nowhere recount his life from
birth to death' (Conze 1959, 34). Ashvaghosha, a monk,
who was patronised by emperor Kanishka, distilled the
Enlightened One's life story from the cycles of legends. The

main sources were the two scriptures, *Mahavastu* and *Lalita Vistara*, both containing anecdotal fragments of his life, but no consistent narrative. Corresponding to the nascent 'personality cult' of the Buddha and the Bodhisattvas, Ashvaghosha accomplished the first biography *per se*, the *Buddha-charita—The Life of the Buddha*. This text, the first great extant work of classical Sanskrit literature (unbelievable as this might sound to those who believe in the 5,000-year-old antiquity of India and Hinduism), was extremely influential in defining perceptions of the Buddha as a person, within the Buddhist fold, as well as beyond. The *Buddha-charita* was not only a highly appreciated poetic hagiography of the historical Buddha, it also added value to Buddhism by enhancing its portability, and thus its reach.

☙

Drifting though the ruins of Charsadda, Takht-i Bahi and Taxila, we might be forgiven for wondering whether the amazing Kushan civilisation was just a mirage, the product of some Buddhist pilgrim's overheated imagination, so far removed is it from today's realities. Pakistan's North West Frontier Province (NWFP) is a remote mountainous area, often invoked as one of the last strongholds of feudal and patriarchal barbarism. However, only 28 kilometres separate Peshawar, the capital of drug-smugglers, gun-runners and CIA trackers, from Pushkalavati, the western centre of the Kushan Empire. This cradle of civilisation is known to have been heavily plundered by high-ranking Pakistan army officers, who must by now own some of the most beautiful antiquities in the world, having supplemented their collections from Taliban sources, who, while they blew up the colossal Buddhas of Bamiyan, put the pagan icons in Afghan museums to a more profitable use. There is now a flow of Gandhara treasures, the result of bombardment archaeology, available for the delectation of museums, private collections and auction houses in the West. The Kushan era contradicts the current perception that tribes, religions and nations are fixed blocs engaged in perpetual conflict with one another: Pashtuns against Tajiks, Muslims against non-believers, Hindus against Muslims, Western rule of law against Oriental feudal custom.

The finds that the charred earth of this region yields, tell a different story, starting with the coins: The Kushan mint-masters, using Alexandrian techniques like their Roman contemporaries, struck gold and copper coinage that variously bore images of the Buddha, of the mother-goddess Nanaia and of Oesho, a new god inspired by Poseidon (see the trident and the bull) and Herakles (see the club), who was soon to make a dramatic career in India as Shiva. The inscriptions were both in Greek and Sanskrit, the emperor styling himself as '*Soter megas*' and as '*Maha-trata*', claiming the divine status of the 'Great Saviour' in two languages. So when Kushan gamblers tossed a coin to decide a wager, the fall of the coin revealed only one side of their intricately multi-layered identity.

Even before the Kushan period, this region had been a web of different cults and practices. The long-established threads of Vedic Brahmanism and Zoroastrianism were competing with newer influences like Buddhism and Greek paganism. At the invitation of the Kushan emperors, Persian Magian priests officiated at the imperial solar and fire cults, at the heart of which stood Mitra-Surya, the sun-god. At the same time, the Kushan rulers extended their aegis to Buddhist monks, fieldworkers of the major proselytising and mobile belief system of the time. These itinerant monks took advantage of such patronage to propagate their ideas throughout the empire and beyond, all the way to Alexandria. Sharing the road with traders, they became adept at linking spiritual merit with mercantile profit. They constructed stupas and *viharas*, reliquary temples and monasteries that became focal points of a new sacred geography. Pilgrimage routes were mapped over caravan highways. The stupas also invited revenue in the form of a mandatory traveller's tax. Princes, smugglers, merchants and artisans all made periodic offerings or endowments to the Buddhist monasteries. 'The devotees, monks or laymen', the Chinese historian Xinru Liu writes, 'were encouraged to worship these stupas with many valuable items, which were easily available from long distance trade. The most important goods were silks, often in the form of banners draped on the stupas, and the Seven Treasures' (Xinru Liu 1998, 13). The seven treasures referred to here mark an ironic development in the history of Mahayana Buddhist practice: how to sanctify the material in the light of the holy, an almost Benedictine problem. The issue was resolved by offering riches as symbolic of the great treasures of the spiritual quest: gold, silver, quartz, lapis lazuli, red coral, pearls and agate became cherished votive offerings, a devotee's pride and a monastery's profit. Significantly, Buddhist Sanskrit texts of this period emphasise worship and donation as ways of achieving merit, over the tripartite path of wisdom, ethical conduct and meditation. But above all, the surplus wealth generated by the stupa economy enabled the flowering of the extraordinary Buddhist art of the Kushan period.

Standard works on Indian history accord the Kushans a couple of cursory pages, skimming over this 'dark period' in a manner similar to that of conservative European historians who used to dismiss the Middle Ages. A. L. Basham (*The Wonder That Was India*) manages to marginalise the Kushans into oblivion. Other authors devote between one and five pages to this period, and even Kulke/Rothermund, who show awareness of the importance of this period, are hasty surveyors (six pages). The Kushans are hustled, with their immediate predecessors and contemporaries, the Indo-Greeks, the Graeco-Bactrians and the Indo-Scythians, into a section bearing some such title as 'The Age of Invasions'. They are presented as brief interlopers between the glories of the Mauryan and the Gupta dynasties, who are regarded as truly and natively 'Indian'.

The popular histories reflect the entrenched positions of the specialists. Since the excavation of the Indo-Greek and Kushan sites began in the 1830s, there have been two equally simplistic and mutually antagonistic interpretations. Colonial historians such as Vincent Smith and W. W. Tarn attempted to prove that the evolution towards higher civilisation in India was due to foreign intervention: the Aryan invasion, the encounter with Greek civilisation, the trade with Rome and so forth. According to this legitimisation mythology, the British were only the most recent of a series of benevolent occupiers. Striking back, nationalist historians repudiated all 'outside' influences as irrelevant, privileging 'native' sources (E. B. Havell, Ananda Kentish Coomaraswamy—neither, incidentally, was Indian). Their argument, elegantly circular, claimed that the 'inside' cultures sought to express 'an Indian spirit' and therefore their sculpture was more truly 'Indian'. Both sides agreed only on one matter, and in this both of them erred: that there were two distinctive and mutually exclusive regional styles in Kushan art, those of Gandhara and Mathura. While in Gandhara the Graeco-Roman morphology supposedly dominated over Indic religious themes, the Mathura style was seen to remain true to its 'national' essence, embodying a stylistic continuity with the prior art of Gangetic India, especially of the Buddhist centres of Bharhut and Sanchi. The colonial British scholars claimed superiority for Gandhara by virtue of its 'European' antecedents, the nationalists insisted that Mathura was the 'native', and therefore the more authentic school. Seen in the clear light of day, however, the two 'styles' have far more mutual affinities than differences. They represent a mix, not only of Indic and Graeco-Roman, but also of Persian, Chinese and Turkic elements. The Buddhas and Bodhisattvas of both styles are robed in variations of the Buddhist *sanghati* as well as the Greek cloaks and tunics known as the *himation*, *chiton* and *palliatus*. To compound the confusion for fans of rigid distinctions, the *sanghati* is often shaped after the Roman toga. The differences are purely morphological (and of course differing from artist to artist, in the handling of plasticity), the Gandhara style preferring a more delicate, the Mathura a more robust figuration. Such variances can reasonably be attributed to contrasting workshop practices and artisanal lineages. However, even the Mathura Buddha is hallowed by a nimbus richly encrusted with vegetal motifs and attendant figures—elements adapted from Persian Zoroastrian iconography. In short, both 'styles' were born of the Kushan confluence: examined over the whole period of Kushan ascendancy, there is ever-increasing interplay between the two. The fierce dispute between art historians is unmasked as a proxy war between colonialism and the Indian freedom struggle, with the scholars involved unfortunately trapped in a misguided *esprit de corps*, on both sides.

But art history is far more eloquent than a discussion of stylistic differences might suggest. The imperial conception of the Kushan rulers, inspired as previously indicated by Persian and Chinese role models, called for a regal representation of the gods. The deity needs a temple just as the king needs a palace—the ruler is expected to be enthroned both on earth as well as in heaven. His person has to reflect power, sovereignty and majesty. Since the Kushan emperors patronised sacred art without denominational prejudice, this new ideology affected all the Indic religions. The Jaina Tirthankaras were previously mere votive figures, central to a tablet stone, but surrounded and nearly overwhelmed by decorative signs of the auspicious—as if one could not trust them to fulfil their duties by themselves. In the Brahmanical tradition there was even less of a precursor. The abstract deities of Vedic belief required, as we have seen, neither temples nor icons. In the earlier Maurya and Shunga periods, small shrines were invariably dedicated to local guardian spirits. 'The mass of the people worshipped ... local genii (Yakshas and Nagas) and feminine divinities of increase, and mother goddesses' (Coomaraswamy 1985, 42). The Vedic gods appeared only on the friezes and panels of the Buddhist complexes that depicted every echelon of divine, human and animal life. The gods were only characters in an architectural narrative, not freestanding cult figures demanding obeisance. The Kushan period gave birth to the single cult figure, and this revolution defines its place in art history far more than disputes over folds and pleats.

The essentialist dogma of many Indologists continues to blind them to confluential realities. The Kushans remain schematically inconvenient. They are too 'foreign' to be fitted into the Hegelian model beloved of the nationalists—the gradual unfolding of the spirit of Indian civilisation, dynasty after dynasty and style after style. As a corollary, all evidence of hybridity is rendered invisible by using the magical tools of cataloguing: the Kushan sculptures, coins and texts are correctly dated, but labelled in vague generalities such as 'Buddhist', 'Early Classical Sanskrit' or 'of Mathura provenance'. Every conjuror tricks his audience by diverting its attention from the decisive action. By imposing their positions onto the past, most scholars have ignored the inextricable weave of sources before their and our eyes, and thus done grave injustice to one of the most luminous examples of cultural accomplishment in history.

By the 4th century CE, the Kushans had dissolved as a great empire, suffering fragmentation into sub-regimes on the eastern side, and defeat at the hands of the Iranian Sassanids on the western. Such major changes of power, to the general understanding, would spell the end of a culture. The last days of an empire, both in literature and film, are imbued with the resonance of apocalypse. Although the defeat sometimes spelled the end for the ruling elite and its favoured way of life, it paradoxically often enabled the losing side to exert a transformative influence on the victorious one—the afterlife of a vanished culture. Thus the influence of a civilisation does not end with its political demise; rather, it lingers on in the bloodstream of succeeding cultures, a pattern as complex and at times cryptic and unpredictable as the recessive genes of the human DNA sequence.

The Kushan Empire could be regarded as a laboratory situation of confluence, close to perfect in its political and social parameters: the mix of ethnicities, shifting borders, absence of internal conflicts, and perhaps most important, an invitation to syncretism extended by an enlightened ruling class.

IV

The Ghetto of the Mind

THE DEATH OF CONFLUENCE AND THE RISE OF EXTERMINATION

The year 1492 is a landmark in human history: in that threshold year, as we all know, as is taught in schools and commemorated with anniversaries and centennials, the Nuremberg cloth merchant Martin Behaim made the first globe. It was marked with 1,100 place names and detailed legends concerning commercial conventions, merchandise and trade routes, as well as miniature portraits of 48 rulers from across the planet. Behaim had just returned from an expedition to West Africa: on his globe, scientific knowledge and mercantile interest chased one another, and made the world go round. It is therefore hardly a coincidence that, just a day or two after this German merchant had presented his new device to Europe's geographers, Christopher Columbus sailed out West to find a way to the East. When the whole world lies literally under your eyes, it is easy to imagine that you can lay hands on it.

Five months after setting sail, Columbus landed in the Bahamas and sent out his Arabic-speaking Jewish translator, Luis de Torres, to ceremonially approach the astonishingly lightly clad locals. Unfortunately, we do not know at what moment, thanks to the linguistic skills of Senor de Torres, it became clear to the Commandante that he had not exactly landed in the East, where everybody, of course, would be expected to speak the universal language of culture—Arabic. Six years later, on the other side of the planet, Vasco da Gama landed near Calicut on the Western Coast of India in 1498. He was met by a Tunisian merchant who greeted him in Spanish: 'May the Devil take you! What brought you here?' Da Gama had only reached India because he had had the foresight to hire an Arab navigator in Malindi (in today's Kenya). Previously, it was Jewish navigational expertise that had helped the Portuguese to reach the Cape of Good Hope, credit for which usually goes to heroes of the 'Age of Exploration' like Prince Henry the Navigator and Bartolomeo Diaz.

'Having expelled all the Jews from Your domains in that same month of January, Your Highnesses command me to go with an adequate fleet to these parts of India (the Americas) … I departed from the city of Granada on Saturday 12 May and went to the port of Palos, where I prepared three ships' (Brotton 2002, 32). Thus Columbus wrote to the royal couple, Ferdinand and Isabella, who had entered the Alhambra ceremonially dressed in 'Moorish' costume, to take the keys of the citadel from the last Nasrid ruler, before he was exiled across the Straits of Gibraltar. Columbus was evidently aware of the connection between the ongoing exorcism within and the first step towards global domination.

His ships sailed from Palos on 3 August; it was the first day of the diaspora from al-Andalus, and the port was crowded with Jews departing from their beloved homeland into a clouded future. So when Columbus reached the New World, there was no other way he could understand it than in the terms of the world he had left behind. The ethnic cleansing of Spain had begun, the Inquisition's totalitarian oppression of dissidence and difference had been going on for more than a decade. People of other colour and conviction were being stigmatised. The Castilian rulers were keen to wipe out all the remnants and memories of al-Andalus. In 1391, a pogrom had been mounted against the Jews in Christian Iberia, especially in Castile; tens of thousands were killed. The survivors fled to Muslim Andalus or converted. In 1412, a royal edict had confined Jews and Muslims to ghettos. In 1480, the Catholic sovereigns had introduced the Inquisition, with the aim of 'cleansing society of non-Christians' and giving more weight to those who could prove that they had been Christians for a long time, and thus free of any deleterious foreign influences. Thousand of libraries were burned, and the ideal of a racially pure Christian propagated. The Inquisition was unrelenting in the attention it paid to every detail, no matter how seemingly trivial or harmless, just in case the Great Satan was hiding there. It banned certain scales in flamenco music, on the grounds that these were the 'work of the Devil'. No doubt the guardians of the Holy Grail were discomfited by the obvious Arab origin of a leap over three semitones. Spaniards even faced arrest for washing themselves, since a daily bath was associated with Islamic standards of hygiene, in the minds of the Catholic authorities (remember the fork!).

The expulsion of the Jews in 1492 was followed, a mere 50 years later, by the expulsion of the Muslims. The lively churning of languages in al-Andalus—Arabic, Castilian, Hebrew and Romance—was over, and translators like de Torres would no longer be required, now that Castilian had been renamed 'Old Christian' or simply 'Cristiano', and imposed as the state language. Those Jews and Muslims who wished to stay were to be baptised, to change their faith, their names and their language, and to forget 800 years of *convivencia*. No wonder the inhabitants of the New World were immediately categorised as aliens, as primitive and of a lower order, and thus to be culturally enslaved or physically annihilated at no risk to the immortal Christian souls of the conquerors. It is symptomatic that, in the 1520s, Cortes compares the houses and the people of Tenochtitlan to 'those of Granada when that city was captured' and refers to the Aztec temples as 'mosques'. And the '*Requirimiento*, the speech read out by Spanish commanders when claiming control over territories and peoples in the New World, was based on the document used to demand the submission of Muslims during the Reconquista. Spain exported its military aggression and religious intolerance ... to the New World' (Brotton 2002, 180).

The rest, unfortunately, is history, and we will never know what kind of cultural encounter might have flowered, had Europe met and interacted with the American civilisations on equal terms, in the spirit of al-Andalus. The Aztecs and the Incas were exterminated just like tens of millions of other inhabitants of the Americas; it is impossible to gauge the exact numbers. When confluence folds up, genocide takes over.

BROTHERS IN THOUGHT: HINDUTVA AND ISLAMISM

Columbus found a Caribbean chieftain and addressed him, through Torres, in a courtly idiom intended for the monarchs of India; six years after this historic fiasco, Vasco da Gama found his way to the court of the Samudrin, the south Indian 'Emperor of the Seas'. To the amusement of the court, da Gama offered this potentate a tribute of glass beads, coral and trinkets. Two years later, his successor Pedro Alvarez Cabral, that brave knight who had crossed the seas bearing the standard of Christ and King, stood before the same monarch and also made a fool of himself—this time, by demanding that the Samudrin expel all Muslims from his domain. A demand that the Indian ruler bluntly refused, observing that his domain was open to all who wished to trade and worship there (Ghosh 1992, 286). Today, Alvarez would receive an enthusiastic embrace from the militants of Hindutva, a movement that has attempted to politicise the historically plural and receptive Hindu sensibility into a narrow, hard-edged identity in the name of safeguarding the essence of Hinduism against the 'historic enemy', Islam.

∞

'To keep up the purity of the nation and its culture, Germany shocked the world by purging the country of the Jews. National pride at its highest has been manifested here,' thunders the ideologue of purity, and the massed legions of his followers cheer. His words are published and circulated immediately, and come to enjoy a wide and growing readership. 'Germany has shown how impossible it is for race and cultures, having differences going to the root, to be assimilated into one united whole,' he continues, and is once more met by applause, his words being quoted in conversation, pamphlets and in graffiti, 'a good lesson for us in Hindustan to learn and profit by.'

Thus spoke M. S. Golwalkar (1906–1973), described reverently as 'Guruji' by his followers (Golwalkar 1939). A bachelor of austere personal habits, with a master's degree in zoology and some years of experience as a sanyasin or monk, he dedicated himself to a lifelong obsession with purifying India of all confluential contamination: Golwalkar was the second Supreme Commander of the Rashtriya Swayamsevak Sangh (RSS) and its most voluminous and influential ideologue. The RSS was founded in Nagpur, near the geographical centre of the Indian subcontinent, in 1925. It had three fundamental aims, which have been openly declared sometimes and at other times carefully toned down. First: to serve as the vanguard of Hindutva, presented as a Hinduism that had been cleansed of all borrowings, encrustations and traces of other traditions (or rather, since Hinduism could not possibly have defiled its true essence in this way, this was a cleansing of popular delusions). Second: to safeguard Indian culture—that is, Hindu culture, since, in the Golwalkarite syllogism, to be Hindu is to be Indian and to be Indian is to be Hindu. Nothing less than the cleansing of non-Hindus from India would guarantee the success of this goal: to Golwalkar, Muslims and Christians were second-class citizens at best; they should not hope for the rights of citizens, which could only belong to Hindus. And why? Because the Hindu is the only one who regards India as the home of his ancestors, the land where his ancestors' temples are, and where his ancestral faith was born. The Muslim looks to Mecca for religious inspiration, and the

Christian to Rome or the Levant. Thus, both are stripped of reasons for belonging to Golwalkar's Hindu *rashtra*, or 'Hindu nation', the establishment of which is the third and long-term aim of the RSS. Unless the misguided see the light of wisdom and become 'Hindu Muslims' and 'Hindu Christians', of course, and practise their religions in accord with the customs and practices of the religious majority. A Castilian argument indeed!

Substitute '*rashtra*' with '*Volk*' and the wellsprings of Golwalkar's thought reveal themselves. While the RSS would like to be viewed as the custodian of a pure, ancient Hinduism—we have already shown how pure, ancient and Hindu this tradition is in the sub-chapter 'Travelling Back in Faith', the RSS worldview is a farrago compounded from German romanticism, Victorian puritanism, *hatha yoga*, and Nazism. From the political interpretation of German romantic thought, the RSS culls the idea that a healthy society is one that can boast a homogenous population, speaking one language and following one religion (in the unreconstructed days when racial discourse was still fashionable, of course, Hindutva was happy to speak of 'Aryan' values, but the racial motif has faded in recent years, since recruitment strategy dictates that the organisation must reach out to the populous 'non-Aryans'). From the curious admixture of Victorian puritanism and *hatha yoga* comes Golwalkar's preoccupation with a life of self-overcoming that makes no concession to the human affections, to sensuous feeling, to desire and even friendship or love, all dismissed as weaknesses that damage the RSS activist's commitment to the holy cause. Only the celibate who blinkers himself to the world of experience, since the cause gives him all the joy he can possibly want, can truly liberate Bharat Mata, 'Mother India', from her chains. And from Sri Adolf Bhagavan, of course, the RSS derives its ideology as well as its methodology in this rather crucial matter: ridding society of the Other within.

Hindutva enters the public sphere in several avatars, nearly all masked acronyms, beginning with the RSS, of course. There are also the BJP (Bharatiya Janata Party, a political party that formed a coalition with ex-socialists and other opportunists, which misruled India from 1996 to 2002), the VHP (Vishwa Hindu Parishad, a pressure group that pours Hindutva propaganda into the world, through speeches, pamphlets, books and websites), and the Bajrang Dal (the SA of Hindutva, a street-fighting outfit that specialises in assaults on movie halls, theatres, concerts, political meetings, or any other venue that hosts activities disapproved of by the Hindutva forces). This plurality of avatars allows Hindutva to play various games, from conspiracy to confrontation, from defensiveness to aggression. All the front organisations of Hindutva are agreed, however, on a millenarian vision of history: to them, British colonialism was only a small episode of relatively benign occupation. The real 'foreign rule' began in 1000 CE, with the first Turkic incursions, and has continued over various sultanates for a thousand years; parts of al-Hind have been re-conquered, but the occupation will not end until the last Muslim has been expelled from the Hindu *rashtra*.

∞

The RSS is a committed supporter of education. It runs a network of schools across India, and in these and the *shakha*s or branches that it has in a great many cities and small towns, children and adolescents are brought up with its doctrines. Operating parallel to the system of secular education, the RSS educational network infuses its communal ideology into pupils at an impressionable age. Its curriculum reduces the complexly woven tapestry of Hindu-Muslim relations to a cartoon-strip narrative of evil Muslim invaders and innocent Hindu victims, destroyed temples and forced conversions, proud owners reduced to slaves in their own land. The real estate metaphor bulks large in Hindutva discourse: Golwalkar compares the Hindu to the owner of a house, and the various minorities to welcome guests, tenants who have outstayed their lease, and squatters who have taken over the house. The Ramjanmabhoomi agitation—which culminated in the destruction of the Babri Masjid, Babar's Mosque, in Ayodhya in 1992—was based on the demand that the site be returned to the Hindus, because it marked the birthplace of Rama, a heroic manifestation of the Divine. Hindutva spokesmen did not react favourably when asked how the Divine, which is the Infinite, could be circumscribed to a birthplace—moreover one that appears, from archaeological evidence, to have hosted Buddhist and Jain shrines as well.

In a re-enactment of the *Reichskristallnacht*, Hindutva's storm-troopers launched a pogrom against the Muslim minority in the state of Gujarat, early in 2002. As in the Germany of the 1930s, the pogrom was motivated both by cultural-nationalist and economic interests, and was meant to achieve the complete annihilation of the minority's economic base as well as its religious and cultural space. 'Rich Muslim homes and business establishments were first systematically looted,' writes the social activist and former senior bureaucrat Harsh Mander. 'Mosques and dargahs [tombs of Sufi saints] were razed, and were replaced by statues of Hanuman and saffron flags. Some dargahs in Ahmedabad city crossings have overnight been demolished and their sites covered with road building material, and bulldozed so efficiently that these spots are indistinguishable from the rest of the road. Traffic now plies over these former dargahs, as though they never existed.' It was very easy for the instigators to recruit a ragged army of part-time killers from the lumpen proletariat of the large cities, who are lured by the promise of loot. But the affluent were not to be outdone, and arrived at the scenes of violence in their shiny limousines, to indulge in some pleasant drive-in looting, lending a hand in an innovative community-building exercise. 'People from well-to-do families were caught on hidden cameras and close-circuit TVs, looting shops before setting them on fire' (*The Hindu*, 5 May 2002).

Gujarat 2002 has infamously been lauded as a 'laboratory' by the genocidal forces of Hindutva. Such is the clinical gloss placed on the systematic slaughter and dispossession of the state's Muslim population, a horror in which the state government, controlled by the BJP was deeply complicit. The cataclysm began with an altercation at the small-town railway station of Godhra on 27 February 2002, during which local Muslims are alleged to have set fire to a train compartment occupied by Hindutva activists: this incident bears every sign of having been mounted by *agents provocateurs*—the Reichstag fire is a shining example for the followers of Sri Adolf Bhagavan—and in a supposedly spontaneous demonstration of outrage across Gujarat,

Muslim-owned properties were put to the torch. The 'spontaneous demonstration' stretched over several weeks. More than 2,000 people were killed, barbarous scenes of rape and butchery enacted, entire neighbourhoods subjected to ethnic cleansing. In the aftermath to this holocaust, homeless Muslims were hustled into refugee camps, where they continue to live even today, 10 years later. Forbidden by unwritten laws to return to their neighbourhoods, these individuals have suffered a loss of citizenship for all practical purposes: they are denied basic amenities and entitlements, and while social sanction withholds livelihood opportunities from them, a Kafkaesque logic based on the possession of proofs of identity, domicile and residence has snatched from many of them the basic right to vote. And who, in any case, would they vote for—when hardly any political leaders came forward to help them in their distress?

The scale of the supposedly retaliatory violence that followed the Godhra incident and the high level of preparedness among the attack squads, with stockpiles of weaponry in position, well-rehearsed communication lines and unrestricted access to demographic data, make it clear that the pogrom was carefully orchestrated. Judicial as well as independent inquiries have demonstrated the shocking extent to which ministers, bureaucrats, police officials and the lower judiciary in Gujarat participated as key actors in the staging of this pogrom, and the manner in which the State's apparatus of law, order and justice had been perverted to serve the bloodlust of the Right. And when the Additional Commissioner of Police in Ahmedabad, one of the worst affected cities, told a team of EU diplomats that every Muslim business in Hindu and mixed areas had been destroyed, he underlined the obvious: those who lament that the 'economic loss in Gujarat was severe', an estimated Rupees 11,000 crore (Euro 2.200 million), overlook that the brunt of this loss was suffered by Muslim traders and businessmen, and that their Hindu competitors stand to gain in the long run. With one stroke, the largest and most economically competitive minority has been expropriated. The anticipation of such gains explains the active cooperation, for instance, between political activists and thugs on the one hand, and on the other, the administration, which supplied the necessary background information, and the construction mafia, which made inroads into high-density areas.

The eyes that were fixed on the profits to be made on new towers, malls and skyscrapers were blind to the shared history they were trampling over, in their haste to realise their dreams. The 180 mosques that were destroyed may have been restricted to the Muslim devout, but the 240 dargahs, shrines to Sufi saints, attracted the devout from all religions—as Sufi shrines do everywhere in India. In Ahmedabad, one of the shrines that was demolished and paved over in a single night was the tomb of Wali Gujarati, among the earliest Urdu poets, a pioneer of the southern Dakhani as well as the modern Gujarati when these were vernaculars—an inspiration to poets of all faiths, who wished to write in the language of the people. The tomb of the musician Ustad Faiyaz Ali Khan was desecrated and wreathed in burning tyres: here was a maestro who had excelled in the rendition of *bhajans*, hymns that are addressed to Hindu deities but which often partake of Sufi ideas. By a fine and multilayered irony, the late Mallikarjun Mansur, a renowned master of classical Indian music and a staunch Hindu, would name as his favourite *bhajan*, one that began with the words *Pratham Allah*, 'Before everything, comes Allah.'

The texture of Indian society has always encouraged communities to develop forms of *convivencia*, since trades, skills, legacies of expertise and bodies of knowledge have been specialised by caste-group and fraternity; thus, social life in India is the result of innumerable social, economic and cultural transactions among different groups. In such a situation, polarisation between groups would be seen as a nightmare rather than a dream. The communal divide was a convenient instrument for the British colonial administration, especially after the Great Revolt of 1857. With census, unequal preferment, separate electorates and a rhetoric of irreconcilable difference among groups, the Empire manipulated the millennial Hindu-Muslim conflict into existence, and ultra-nationalists in both communities took it up with enthusiasm, turning a fiction into a self-fulfilling prophecy. The post-colonial nation-states of India and Pakistan, Midnight's Twins, each menaced by unresolved internal strife and each obsessed with the negation of the other, are the result.

What makes the situation of Muslims in India intolerable is the long-running Hindu right-wing propaganda campaign which insists that they have been beneficiaries of preferment and special treatment, with a sequence of secular governments allegedly having 'appeased' them, and that they are all actual or potential terrorists owing allegiance to Pakistan. As against this, the findings of the Justice Rajinder Sachar Committee has irrefutably revealed the lack of educational and employment opportunities, and the consequently attenuated life choices, that confront the majority of Indian Muslims. Official appeasement, such as it is, has been extended to a dangerously oppressive clerical elite that has only contributed to the Muslim community's backwardness and ghettoisation.

When you push the Other into a ghetto, you push yourself into a corresponding ghetto too, even if yours is as large as a nation or a continent. Unfortunately, no territory is too large to be squeezed into the self-imprisonment of exclusionist or annihilatory politics.

∽◦◦∾

Golwalkar was not by any means the only non-Western intellectual who found inspiration in dangerous Western authoritarian ideologies, and attempted the transformation of a traditional religion into a modern political weapon. Colonial subjects everywhere in the late 19th and early 20th centuries believed that their degradation was due to a loss, variously, of moral fibre, intellectual stamina or physical courage—a softening of the consciousness that demanded to be overcome by discipline, order and stern assertiveness. The moving spirits of Islamism, which is the counterpart of Hindutva in Islam, furnish us with trajectories of ideological development that are parallel to Golwalkar's.

One of the intellectual fathers of Islamism was Syed Abul A'ala Maududi (1903–1979), the founder of the Jama'at-i-Islami. Contrary to the popular assumption that Islamism was created and is sustained by backward-looking men educated narrowly in seminaries and bereft of any experience of the world beyond the Koran and the Hadith, Maududi was not trained as an *'alim* in the traditional manner. He was an Indian journalist and writer who, after the Partition of British India, became a staunch champion of an Islamic state in Pakistan.

The strongest influence on Maududi came from the writings of Alexis Carrel (1873–1944), a pioneer of transplant surgery who won the Nobel Prize and also supported the Vichy regime, dying shortly before being tried as a war criminal. In his bestselling 1935 testament, *Man, the Unknown*, Carrel advocated the use of eugenics to cultivate an intellectual elite that could guide society towards progress, and the use of genetic selection to grade society into a hierarchy of classes defined by specifically accentuated characteristics. A Darwino-Lombrosian approximation of caste, one could say and dismiss it—after all, crackpots are entitled to their own confluences too—but Carrel's storehouse of pathologies was not quite exhausted. He was an energetic advocate of euthanasia, as the best solution by which society could rid itself of its genetically inferior, mentally feeble, insane, criminal or otherwise undesirable members. Indeed, in his view, they did not qualify for membership at all. In the mid-1930s, before the Nazis had applied themselves seriously to the Final Solution, Monsieur le Doctor Carrel was promoting the use of gas chambers for this noble purpose. His name may have sunk into ignominy in scientific circles, but Carrel's political descendants have enshrined his memory: Jean-Marie le Pen has hailed him as 'the first environmentalist', apparently for promoting natural harmony, and his works are religiously read at the training camps of the National Front.

'Carrel's animadversions on the "corruptions" of modern living found their way into Maududi's denunciation of the West as a sewer of vice and wickedness,' writes Malise Ruthven. 'Impressed by the totalitarian movements in Russia, Italy and Germany, he compared Islam favourably with Communism and Fascism as a movement with the potential to mobilise the masses. The Jama'at-i-Islami, with him as *amir* (commander), had more than a hint of Führerprinzip about it' (Ruthven 2002, 69). Grafting Trotsky's emphasis on the permanent revolution onto the pious Islamic hope that the entire world would someday accept the revelation of Mohammed, Maududi 'argued that jihad was the ultimate political struggle for the whole of humankind' (Ruthven 2002, 70). Indeed, in Maududi's West-inspired hands, the Islamic idea of the jihad—which had until then borne the connotation of an individual's spiritual struggle against temptation and indulgence—took on the political meaning of a guerrilla war of the righteous against the unjust. Trotsky may have fallen to an assassin in Mexico, but his spirit was to live on in the House of Islam, unacknowledged but influential.

❦

Like Maududi, the Egyptian scholar Sayyid Qutb (1906–1966), arguably the most influential theoretician of Islamism, was not a seminary product either. As a young man, Qutb—who was executed for his teachings by the Nasser government, teachings that continue to inspire the *mujahiddin* today—had been a member of the modernist Diwan group of writers, which followed English literary models. He read voraciously in translation, established himself as a novelist and literary critic, and acquired a considerable knowledge of European literature and culture. Qutb became disillusioned with

Egyptian nationalism, which had involved collaboration with the British during World War II, and also felt let down by the large-scale settlement of European Jews in Palestine, which he saw, not inaccurately, as a British ploy to move in a permanent ally in the region while keeping the nascent Arab states in a permanent condition of unease. Qutb joined in the agitation against the pro-British Egyptian government. In 1948, the year in which the state of Israel was formally established, he obtained a government grant to study the American educational system. The nearly two years that he spent in Greeley, Colorado, nurtured in him a profound antipathy towards the social and cultural life of the USA. He hated jazz and the free mixing of the sexes; he hated what he saw as the uninhibited behaviour of women in public; indeed, his inability to deal with women as independent human beings explains why, like Golwalkar, he remained a lifelong bachelor. Having been subjugated to a colonial perspective on the native, Qutb was only able to respond by mirroring this distrustful and selective way of seeing the world. Unlike Ibn Batuta and Ibn Khaldun, and many other open-minded Arab travellers and social scientists of earlier times, who were untainted by colonial subjugation, Qutb travelled in the West as a suspicious and resentful observer, and detested the Westernisation of Egyptian society. He answered the Orientalism that he had suffered, with an equal and opposite Occidentalism.

Qutb's concepts were 'rooted in a Romantic ideal of the aesthetic sublime', owing more to thinkers of the Idealist tendency such as Kant and Coleridge than to traditional Islamic philosophy (Ruthven 2002, 82). In his volatile mix of pessimism at the state of his culture, optimistic belief in the renovation of the collective by extreme acts of self-assertion, his desire to break down the idols of conventional political wisdom, he drew inspiration from Nietzsche, Kierkegaard and Heidegger, rather than the Koran or the Hadith. His Nietzsche-like commitment to 'philosophising with a hammer', in particular, did not please the authorities. In 1954, he was arrested on the charge of complicity in an assassination attempt on Nasser; while in prison, he wrote some of his most influential works, among them, 'Signposts on the Road', a tract that has been compared to Lenin's 'What Is To Be Done'.

The collapse of the Soviet Union and the swift absorption of the states under its umbrella into the Western system of patronage can blind us to the epochal importance of the Bolshevik Revolution of 1917 to the oppressed of the colonial world. In Egypt as in India, the Soviet triumph was greeted as a model, and whether acknowledged as an influence or not, its theory and strategy entered the imagination of thinkers of very different orientation. If Maududi internalised the teachings of Imam Trotsky, Qutb drank at the fountain of Lenin-sarai. Qutb's model of an Islamist vanguard as the strategy by which to secure victory against Jahiliyah, hedonism, was clearly derived from Lenin's conception of an avant-garde that would lead the working class and eventually symbolise, and more than symbolise, the 'dictatorship of the proletariat'. In Leninist spirit, Qutb forcefully rejected the view, held by almost all the *ulema*, that jihad is purely spiritual or defensive. Instead, he defied Islamic tradition and insisted on the militant and offensive interpretation of jihad. Qutb's attitude was shaped by the exigencies of responding to what he saw as the intellectual occupation by the West of Islamic thought. Feeling compelled to emancipate himself from this predicament, he accused fellow Muslims who upheld the spiritual interpretation of jihad of being 'apologetic and defeatist, of succumbing to the "wily attacks of the Orientalists", who distort the concept of Islamic jihad' (Ruthven 2002).

❦

For the greater part of the four centuries since Iran became a fully Shi'a country, its theologians and jurists have spent their lives in study and teaching: their worldview was quietist and they had deliberately abjured any involvement in politics, strange as it may seem to those who associate Shi'a Iran with fire-breathing ayatollahs who are quick to dispense fatwahs against infidels and apostates. In the world of Islam more generally, also, a clear line was drawn between the mosque and the palace. Thus, for instance, Ayatollah Khomeini's invention of the *vilaya-i faqih*, the 'mandate of the jurist', was a radical departure from the Islamic, and certainly the Shi'a, custom of quietist scholarship: if the *falasifa* could claim the mantle of the Platonic philosopher-king, why can't the *ulema* create the throne of the Persian jurist-king, he seemed to be asking.

Khomeini, who spent time in exile in Iraq and France, spent many years formulating his thoughts on the subject of the most just and legitimate government for an Islamic country. At the same time, during the 1960s and 1970s, many socialist or Communist intellectuals in Islamic countries had rediscovered the emancipatory potential of Islam while transfusing into their practice of a politicised Islam such concepts from the Left corpus as the revolution, the avant-garde, consciousness-raising and mass-mobilisation. Sociologists and critics of consumerist capitalism like the Iranian Ali Shari'ati (1933–1977), whose teachings provided the inspiration for the first, secular phase of the Iranian Revolution in 1978, openly asserted the need to cull the best elements from the Islamic and the Left tradition, and declared that society and God were the same.

∽◦∾

In this context, we must not overlook the fact that both Sayyid Qutb and Syed Abul A'ala Maududi also published works of Islamic religious scholarship. Both wrote books of *tafsir*, the exegesis of the Koran, which rank among the most influential 20th-century contributions to this discipline. *In the Shade of the Qur'an*, Qutb's four-volume commentary, 'has greatly influenced numerous Muslims, especially the younger generation, and particularly in the Middle East' (von Denffer 1983, 141), while Maududi's *Tafhim al-Qur'an* has held a similar importance for Muslim scholars in the Indian subcontinent. But the fact remains that neither Maududi nor Qutb was a traditionalist. And in this, too, they are astonishingly similar to Golwalkar, whose worldview has little in common with those of the Vedas, the Upanishads, the Bhagavad Gita or the Puranas. Maududi, Qutb and Golwalkar share a number of themes and positions: all three believe that their respective societies, cultures or religions are sunk in apathy or iniquity; that this is the outcome both of colonial oppression and native weakness; that this situation can be overcome by focused acts of self-regeneration through revolutionary, even violent means; that an avant-garde is necessary to lead the way for the rest of society; that no prisoners can be taken, for the entire terrain in question, whether India or the House of Islam or even the world, must be reclaimed for the Pure while the impure must be annihilated. The schemas of Hindutva and of Islamism are counter-modern, for although they oppose the modernity of the West, they align themselves genealogically with concepts of revolutionary theory, strategy and organisation that emanate from within the 19th- and early 20th-century West. The intolerance and violence of Hindutva and Islamism owe more to the global dissemination of modern Western thought than to intrinsic elements of Hindu and Islamic belief respectively. This is why it is a mistake to describe Hindutva and Islamism as 'fundamentalist', since neither worldview refers to any 'fundamental' aspects of the religious canon and history in whose name it speaks. Exactly like the Christian Right—which we have omitted here only for reasons of space—both Hindutva and Islamism are ideologies, the outcome of apprenticeships served by colonial subjects in the workshops of Communism, Nazism, nihilism and existentialism.

DEFINING THE ENEMY: ISLAMOCLASM

How come Hollywood movies never get it right? Not once, not out of respectful diligence and not even by chance. They never show the *salat*, the Islamic prayer, the way it is practised. In *Executive Decision*, a ludicrous thriller with Kurt Russell and Steven Seagal, the terrorists indulge in bizarre aerobics when praying; in *Black Hawk Down*, the *fajr*, the pre-dawn prayer, is performed as the sun rises dramatically over the horizon; in *Spy Game*, the prayers are being conducted while the *azaan*, the call to prayer, still rings out. In most films, the choreography of standing and kneeling—the *rakas* of the *salat*—is all wrong. The prayer is never shown to be dignified, never beautiful, never meaningful. Quite the opposite: it is usually presented as a ridiculous, outlandish exercise, appropriate to the savages who are about to threaten the US cosmology and who will, after hours of chases and shootouts, be slain by the Marines. The Islamic prayers as shown in these films are fictitious and any resemblance to reality is purely coincidental.

Hollywood's attitude reflects the Islamoclasm that has taken hold of the public sphere in North America and Europe, and which lays out broad, unquestioned certainties about the nature and history of Islam. Certainties that are as dogmatic as the supposed dogmas that they set out to oppose. The critique-by-media of Islam claims to defend certain 'core Western values', which are founded on the principles of the Enlightenment and assumed to lie at the base of all civilised discourse. Interpreted correctly, these core Western values enshrine the method of radical doubt and a corresponding receptiveness to entertaining various points of view before reaching a conclusion, thus leading to an *Öffentlichkeit*, or public sphere, where individuals may freely exchange and compare their views and opinions. This is central to Enlightenment philosophy—all the way from Spinoza and Descartes to Habermas and Foucault. The method of radical doubt helps us to unmask religion as ideology, to examine the overt practices and concealed motives of ideology, the manner in which it masks a power structure and the interests of a dominant class. The receptiveness to various points of view allows us to comprehend a thought process, a philosophy or a historical archive in all its density and multiplicity, with meanings both visible and concealed, with manifest effects and latent possibilities. And an *Öffentlichkeit* gives us the luxury of considering various theories and opinions on any subject, while we form our own.

Unfortunately, the current rhetoric of the West in relation to Islam proceeds in complete contravention of this heritage. By demonising Islam, it falls victim to the mystification, closure and lack of nuance that it challenges in the Other. And thus, it betrays the Enlightenment. By contrast, to demand a perspective on Islam in all its complexity is it to defend the Enlightenment—in the tradition of the great Voltaire, who was among the first to propose a reasonable position towards Islam. He presented Islam as a praiseworthy rational religion in *Les Moeurs et l'esprit des nations*, pointing out that it had always been more tolerant than Christianity. And in his *Philosophical Dictionary*, Voltaire answered the demonising calumnies that decried Islam as a pursuit of sensuality: 'Canons, monks, vicars even, if a law were imposed on you not to eat or drink from four in the morning till ten at night, during the month of July, when Lent came at this period... if you had to make a pilgrimage into the burning desert; if it were enjoined on you to give at least two and a half per cent of your income to the poor; if, accustomed to enjoy possession of eighteen women, the number were cut down suddenly by fourteen; honestly, would you dare call that religion sensual?' Yet even Voltaire deployed the Prophet as an allegorical stand-in for the Church in 'Fanaticism, or Mahomet the Prophet' (1741), a play that targeted ecclesiastical tyranny: the allegory was read accurately and angrily by the establishment in his own day, but in late 2005, with the controversy around the Danish cartoons raging fiercely, some Muslims in France protested when a staging of the play was announced. The context had changed, and ironically, Voltaire, who had supported the claims of Islam against Christianity, now appeared to be as much of an Islamoclast as the cartoonist who had lampooned the Prophet in Denmark.

In this changed context, Islam is viewed as a regressive, intolerant religion that demands submission of its followers and commands violence against those who do not follow it. The general image is of a faith that is backward-looking and self-denyingly austere; that swaddles its women in bulky robes when it isn't killing them for defying the family patriarch in matters of love, sex and marriage. As a matter of record, nowhere in the Koran or the Hadith are women ordered to cover themselves from head to toe; as for the so-called 'honour killings' of Muslim women by their families, this has no basis in Islam whatsoever, and arises from the persistence of tribal customs in an embattled contemporary situation where the individual woman's choices have expanded too rapidly for the regressive elements within the family. And as for tolerance, between the 15th and the 17th centuries, the movement of refugees was from west to east, as the Ottomans offered 'a degree of tolerance without precedence or parallel in Christian Europe. Each religious community was allowed the free practise of its religion. ... While ultimate power remained in Muslim hands, non-Muslims controlled much of the economy, and were even able to play a part of some importance in the political process' (Lewis 2002, 34).

The Nobel laureate V. S. Naipaul and others have popularised the idea that contact with Islam has been catastrophic for other cultures—that Islam has wiped out all signs of the cultures it has supplanted, that Islam is an unfinished project that is only waiting for an opportunity for world domination. This is no more than a projection of the aims and methods of European colonialism. We have only to recall that, after centuries of Islamic political dominance, Muslims in India remain a minority and Hinduism flourishes. We have only to point to the beautifully sculpted stone Ganeshas and Garudas that abound in Muslim-majority Indonesia, not to mention the mellifluous Sanskrit names that Indonesia's Muslims bear: Meghawati, Sudarsano, Sukarno, all laden with Hindu mythic associations. And the Buddhist temple-complex of Borobudur stands in splendour, damaged by an earthquake but still a symbol of national pride.

But the texture of historical detail is irksome to those who prefer the contours of their history to be clear-cut. It won't do to confuse the Marines. As Bush the Younger said, in his oration after 9/11, he would launch a crusade against the enemy. That he was flanked by the US capital's leading Christian and Jewish clerics was doubtless, as in the movies, purely coincidental. The President of the USA was not merely recording a lapse in taste in his speech, but also offering testimony to the continuing power of a crude but powerful idea. The crusade remains a template, a legal and political instrument, a powerful idea and inexhaustible source of mobilising metaphors—an endless source of myth, polemic, self-vindication, apologia, prejudice, emergency justice and misunderstanding, which can be instrumentalised time and again, when the situation demands it. But the situation demands it only when the authority of the powerful has been challenged. By contrast, no minutes of silence were maintained for the victims of the Rwandan genocide; no candlelight vigils were held in their memory, no celebrity-endorsed prayer meetings were convened. On the contrary, the shameful involvement of functionaries of the Roman Catholic Church in the genocide was glossed over: no commentator was inspired to publish vicious diatribes against Christianity as a cultural system that regularly breeds bloodthirsty maniacs. But let's not forget that we are only talking of a million dead blacks. Humankind has lived through worse times, but rarely through more hypocritical ones.

THE NONSENSE MANTRAS OF OUR TIMES

As befits an age of hypocrisy, our times resound with the rattling of pebbles in the empty canisters that pass for great ideas. One of these is the thesis of the 'clash of civilisations', originally coined by the long-time observer of Islam, Bernard Lewis, who has regressed from empathetic interest to spiteful exasperation with the people, the religion and the societies on which he has lavished scholarly attention for almost six decades. Beginning his career as the young British scholar who was excited and honoured at being the first Westerner to be granted access to the Ottoman imperial archives in the 1950s, Lewis now reigns as the patriarch of Middle Eastern studies in North America. His belief in a sort of democracy from above and outside as the best solution to an Islamic society's problems—i.e. send in the Marines, knock off the troublemakers who currently rule the place, and replace them with a Western-style government run by people you can trust, and who deliver the oil—has passed into official wisdom, being the ground on which the Bush administration erected its doctrine of 'regime change' in Afghanistan and Iraq. The same vision informed the Obama administration's support of the NATO operation in Libya during 2011, which brought about the downfall of Colonel Qadhafi's government and its replacement by a transitional authority clearly guided by Islamist interests. Presumably, in years to come, this Lewisite vision will influence the US approach to Iran and Syria as well. The key element of the Lewisite vision, that of a 'clash of civilisations', has been picked up by Samuel Huntington and turned into a popular catchphrase to justify the War against Terror, which is a barely veiled War against Islam.

Briefly stated, the Lewis-Huntington thesis (or rather, the Sorokin-Toynbee-Lewis-Huntington thesis, since it has a genealogy of its own, leading back to such revisitations of Ibn Khaldun's cyclical analysis of power and decline as Sorokin's and such justifications of imperialism as Arnold Toynbee's schema of antagonistic civilisational blocs) is that humankind is divided into 'eight or nine' cultural-political blocs arbitrarily defined as 'civilisations'. The thesis emphasises the fault-lines among these 'civilisations', which are seen to exist in a state of conflict based on profoundly distinct cultural values. In Huntington's view, the great clash of our times, which takes the place of the Cold War face-off between the USA and the USSR, is that between Islam and the West. After September 11, Huntington has popularly and uncritically been hailed as the prophet of the age.

Huntington's account is riddled with inconsistency and self-contradiction. He tells us that a civilisation is 'a cultural entity ... with villages, regions, ethnic groups, nationalities, religious groups ... distinct cultures at different levels of cultural heterogeneity.' Furthermore, a civilisation is 'the highest cultural grouping of people and the broadest level of cultural identity people have short of that which distinguishes humans from other species. It is defined both by common objective elements, such as language, history, religion, customs, institutions, and by the subjective self-identification of people.' Therefore civilisation is 'the broadest level of identification with which [an individual] intensely identifies.' This element of self-identification itself contradicts the determinist mainstay of the savant's argument, unless choice is exercised as the willing suspension of choice. Distinctively Western, according to Huntington, are Christianity, democracy, pluralism, individualism and rule of law. We have already seen where the philosophical sources, the personal examples, the mythic infrastructure and the scaffolding of debate that made all these possible lie—namely, in the confluential world of Mediterranea, in al-Andalus, in Arab Aristotelianism, and in that loop of travelling thoughts, stories and manuscripts which crosses blithely from one society to another, seemingly unaware of the supposedly absolute fault lines between civilisational blocs. As to the rule of law, the Sharia was introduced as a universal system of justice, to replace all the variations and uncertainties of tribal custom, whether one agrees with all its provisions or not. And as for democracy, surely even Huntington has heard of the basic democratic structures of many so-called primitive societies, like the autocephalic systems in Africa, and the Nations of the Iroquois.

∞

The truth is somewhat less dramatic, if no less violent, and has more to do with fundamental differentials of economic and political power than with fundamental cultural differences. Civilisations are marvellous hybrids: they have never been pure, self-consistent entities. Historically, they have evolved through exchange and synthesis, through the encounter of different races, religions and philosophies. What is of interest, in the study of civilisations, is not the differences that hold people apart, but the heritage that people are able to share across borders. A more tenable view than the 'clash of civilisations' is that the battle-lines run through societies, not between civilisations or nation-states. A US pacifist, who believes in the necessity of social justice, is worlds apart from an American investment banker, whose clients include Lockheed and Unocal, and who believes that each man is master of his own destiny. An urbane West European, who practises yoga, has a deeply informed interest in African art, listens to reggae, and travels the world in search of cultural inspiration, is equidistant from both the West European skinhead and the Bajrang Dal storm-trooper.

Unfortunately, the assumptions of the West, which are based on binary models, continue to be projected upon the former colonised world, often with the devastating effect of the self-fulfilling prophecy. The worst example of this tendency may be summed up as the 'principle of ethnicity as the basis of political conflict'. Put to excellent use by the Western powers in such situations of conflict as Lebanon and Rwanda, this principle was introduced into the Afghanistan debate, immediately following the flight of the Taliban regime from Kabul and the entry of the Northern Alliance into the Afghan capital on 13 November 2001. For the notion of the tribe is accompanied by the stereotypes of primitive behaviour: barely had the Northern Alliance marched into Kabul, when the Western media came abuzz with loose talk of 'revenge killings' and 'warlordism' (the US Air Force's killing of Afghan civilians was not, apparently, to be categorised under the former rubric; and the strategists at the Pentagon, calibrating the precise degree of offensive force, were not warlords, since Cheney did not favour a turban and Rice did not wear the *hijab*).

This divisive principle came in handy once again, during the occupation of Iraq that began on 20 March 2003, when the US-led invaders destroyed the multiethnic network mobilised by the Ba'ath Party, admittedly under Sunni domination, and emphasised the supposed differences between Shi'a, Sunni, Kurd, Marsh Arab and Chaldean Christian, as though these were absolute and formative. Any discord and violence among these groups was promptly attributed to the centuries of mutual suspicion and hatred that is alleged to have kept them apart even before the occupiers stepped in. The actual causes were the power struggle precipitated by the fall of the Iraqi government, the destruction of infrastructure and the creation of famine-like conditions by the previous embargo, the carefully unequal distribution of patronage, largesse, and security to various constituencies by the occupying forces, and a guinea-pigisation to prove the most unbalanced theories of neoliberalism.

It is now well known that 'tribes' were often invented by anthropologists ranging unfamiliar terrain while driven by a classificatory mania (the early British explorers of Australia, eager to find a paradise in the antipodes, even invented whole terrains of river, forest and pasture; naturally, the aboriginals who marred this idyll were soon rounded up, exterminated or their children handed over to good Western Christian settlers, so that their souls could be saved). Never mind that the identities on the ground were often fluid or blurred, with language defining one affiliation, clan system a second, religious sect a third, and political allegiance a fourth. Also, identities and allegiances could change, leaving the already inaccurate taxonomy further behind; but the so-called tribal differences, once established by the Western knowledge system, were exploited by the colonial power system through the honourable imperialist formula: Divide and rule. Until the Soviet occupation, ethnicity played a minor role in the modern Afghan consciousness. After 1978, however, the foreign powers that interfered in Afghanistan (and kept the civil war going) raised and supported militias that were organised on ethnic lines. Within this scheme, the success of the Taliban was due only to the fact of a vacuum in Pashtun representation. Nevertheless, Kabul's Pashtun population welcomed the predominantly Tajik and Uzbek troops of the Northern Alliance after the Taliban were overthrown, apparently reconciled to this latest change despite the rather brutal record of the Northern Alliance when it last held the Afghan capital. As the foreign powers have continued to insist on bizarre ethno-federalist structures with quotas, veto rights and reservation proportional to clout in the post-Taliban scenario, Afghanistan's future has spiralled into a catastrophe. The worst sufferers in this scenario have been the women of Afghanistan: once proud of their progressive achievements, they have lost their independence utterly, and are held to ransom by the whims of patriarchal warlords. So much for the interference of a West committed to democracy and the rights of the individual, to pluralism and the rule of law.

The world will always be threatened by forces that instrumentalise differences. What is needed is a vision of unity, a vision of how the Afghan people can invent themselves beyond the quagmire into which they have been thrust by superpower politics and the cynical games of regional powers. Precisely the same conclusion applies to the continuing crisis in Iraq.

∞

The perception of the Other, on the part of a West that sees itself as the driving principle of the world, has veered between universalism and relativism (or multiculturalism as it is known in one version). While the universalists derive their notions of a common human nature and general human rights from an attitude of superiority, a form of cultural arrogance that would bring deviants into line, the relativists are limited by their perception of cultures being intrinsically and inherently different from one another, and therefore, eventually, incapable of meeting on common ground. From neither standpoint can the West achieve understanding of a society or a tendency that proceeds from strikingly different assumptions to its own, and conflicts are only to be expected. And indeed, the relativist position, which may sometimes appear to be more respectful of the Other, is by far the more tragic of the two options. For many relativists, not only is each culture unique unto itself, 'but people's thoughts, feelings and motivations are radically different from one culture to another. It follows then that any attempt to generalise about either culture or human nature must be false or trivial unless it is confined to people who live in a specific cultural system. As these relativists have said, it necessarily follows that if peoples' minds vary so much from one culture to another, Western science is only a culturally specific form of ethnoscience, not a universally valid way of verification or falsification. In this perspective, a person from another culture remains the "Other", forever incomprehensible' (Edgerton 1992).

This also justifies the old maxim: One rule for the West, another for the others. This illiberal attitude within the liberal tradition goes back to J. S. Mill, that fountainhead of European liberalism who opposed the idea of self-determination for the world's colonised peoples. This colonialist ideology has not yet been eradicated from the Western mind, and though we have achieved a sort of globalism in terms of mass communications and trade, we are still a long way from evolving a global ethics, that would guide the relations among nations and peoples. Without being as philosophically ambitious as the Advaita, Plotinus or Ibn Rushd, we would have achieved a great change if we could accept that the same essence animates every human life, which should therefore be held to have the same and equal value, irrespective of race, region, nation or religion.

Our search in this book has been for the connections, which have sometimes gone underground or blurred into background noise, that have brought people together across the so-called fault lines between civilisations. Indeed, we have tried to show that civilisations, far from mutually exclusive divisions, are constantly weaving through one another. In quest of a vision of community, based on ideals of mutuality and solidarity found in teachings seemingly as far apart as the Avatamsaka-sutra and utopian philosophy, we come to the Buddhist image of the world as the Net of Indra. Every knot in this net, where strings cross, is an individual; and each of these individuals reflects all the others around him or her. Individuals come into an awareness of themselves through their relations with each other, and not in a limbo of exaggerated self-importance to the exclusion of the needs of strangers. When we look at ourselves in the Net of Indra, we are not only the selves who inhabit our own bodies, but also a series of reflections and possibilities —all the minds we could savour, all the bodies we could transit through, all the imaginations that could enrich ours. The citadel is a safe place to be on occasion, but eventually it suffocates you: it is the ghetto that you make for yourself, as we have shown, when you force others into ghettos. Far better to be on the routes of the pilgrims and traders, storytellers and troubadours, there to find humankind's true inheritance of wisdom: which is the realisation that cultures do not engage in conflict but flow together, which is why we must reject those who whip up our passions in the name of difference and conscript us into the global machine of war. We conclude with a syllogism of our own: to embrace culture is to renounce conflict, to renounce conflict is to embrace culture.

Bibliography

PRIMARY SOURCES (RELIGIOUS TEXTS)

Holy Bible. New Revised Standard Version. Old and New Testament. Oxford 2001.

Sacred Books of the Jews. Harry Gersh (ed.). New York 1972.

The Gathas of Zarathushtra: Hymns in Praise of Wisdom. Piloo Nanavutty (ed.). Ahmedabad 2008.

The Zend Avesta (Sacred Books of the East). F. Max Mueller (ed.). London 2001.

The Bhagavad Gita. Translated by Eknath Easwaran. Harmondsworth 1988.

The Rig Veda. Translated by Wendy Doniger O'Flaherty. Harmondsworth 1982.

The Upanishads. Translated by Eknath Easwaran. Harmondsworth 1989.

Buddhist Scriptures. Edward Conze (ed.). Harmondsworth 1959.

The Dhammapada. Translated by Eknath Easwaran, Notes by Stephen Ruppenthal. Harmondsworth 1988.

Mahavastu. Translated by J. J. Jones. London 1952.

The Voice of the Buddha, Lalitavistara Sutra. Translated by Gwendolyn Bays. Berkeley 1983.

Al-Qur'an. Translated by Ahmed Ali. Princeton 1994.

PRIMARY SOURCES (SECULAR TEXTS)

Poems of Arab Andalusia. Translated by Cola Franzen. San Francisco 1989.

Arabic Andalusian Casidas. Translated by Joan Penelope Cope. Kent 1953.

Das Wunder von al-Andalus. Übersetzt von Georg Bossong. München 2005.

Three Abbasid Poets. Birds through a Ceiling of Alabaster. Translated by G. B. H. Wightman & A. Y. al-Udhari. Harmondsworth 1975.

Gesta Romanorum. Ausgewählt und eingeleitet von Hermann Hesse. Frankfurt 1978.

Die Trobadors. Leben und Lieder. Übersetzt von Franz Wellner. Bremen 1942.

SECONDARY SOURCES

Ali, Hazrat, *Living and Dying with Grace.* Translated by Thomas Cleary. Boston 1996.

Appiah, Kwame Anthony, *Cosmopolitanism. Ethics in a World of Strangers.* New York 2006.

Arberry, A. J., *The Spiritual Physick of Rhazes.* London 1950.

Armstrong, Karen, *Muhammad. A Biography of the Prophet.* London 1991.

____, *Islam: A Short History.* New York 2000.

Asin y Palacios, Miguel, *La Escatologia musulmana en la 'Divina Comedia'.* Madrid 1919.

____, *Dante y el Islam.* Madrid 1927.

____, *Islam and the Divine Comedy.* Translated by Harold Sunderland. London 1968.

Averroes, *Averroes on Plato's Republic.* Translated by Ralph Lerner. Ithaca 2005.

____, *Faith and Reason in Islam. Averroes' Exposition of Religious Arguments.* Translated by Ibrahim Najjar. Oneworld 2002.

Baier, Lothar, *Die große Ketzerei: Verfolgung und Ausrottung der Katharer durch Kirche und Wissenschaft*. Berlin 1991.

Barber, Benjamin R., *Jihad Vs McWorld: Terrorism's Challenge to Democracy*. New York 2001.

Bartlett, Robert, *The Making of Europe. Conquest, Colonization and Cultural Change 950-1350*. Princeton 1993.

Bitterli, Urs, *Alte Welt—neue Welt. Formen des europäisch-überseeischen Kulturkontaktes 15–18. Jahrhunderts*. München 1992.

Bhabha, Homi K., *The Location of Culture*. London 1994.

Blurton, T. Richard, *Hindu Art*. London 1992.

Burton, Richard, *King Vikram and the Vampire: Classic Hindu Tales of Adventure, Magic, and Romance*. London, 1893, rpt. Rochester, Vt., 1992.

Boon, James A., *Affinities and Extremes*. Chicago 1990.

Bopearachchi, Osmund, 'On the So-called Earliest Representation of Ganesa', in Marie-Francoise Boussac & Jean-Francois Salle (eds), *Athens, Aden, Arikamedu: Essays on the Interrelationships Between India, Arabia and the Eastern Mediterranean*. New Delhi 1995.

Brotton, Jerry, *The Renaissance Bazaar: From the Silk Road to Michelangelo*. Oxford 2002.

Burkert, Walter, *Die Griechen und der Orient*. München 2003.

Butterworth, Charles E., *Averroes' Three Short Commentaries on Aristotle's 'Topics', 'Rhetoric' and 'Poetics'*. Studies in Islamic Philosophy and Science. New York 1977.

Caglar, Gazi, *Der Mythos vom Krieg der Zivilisationen*. München 1997.

Campbell, Joseph, *The Masks of God* Vol. IV. Creative Mythology. New York 1968.

Cardini, Franco, *Europa und der Islam*. München 2000.

De Cervantes, Miguel, *Leben und Taten des scharfsinnigen Edlen Don Quixote von La Mancha: Übersetzt von Ludwig Tieck*. Zürich 1987.

Charles, R. H., *The Chronicle of John, Bishop of Nikiu*, translated from Zotenberg's Ethiopic Text (1916). Merchantville NJ 2007.

Chaudhuri, K. N., *Trade and Civilisation in the Indian Ocean: An Economic History from the Rise of Islam to 1750*. Cambridge 1984.

Chomsky, Noam, *Rogue States: The Rule of Force in World Affairs*. New Delhi 2000.

Choueiri, Youssef M., *Islamic Fundamentalism* (revised edition). London 1997.

Cimino, Rosa Maria (ed.), *Ancient Rome and India*. New Delhi 1994.

Clark, Peter, *Zoroastrianism, An Introduction to an Ancient Faith*. Sussex 1999.

Cohn, Norman, *The Pursuit of the Millennium: Revolutionary Millenarians and Mystical Anarchists of the Middle Ages*. London 1970.

Colley, Linda, *Captives. Britain, Empire and the World 1600–1850*. London 2002.

Constable, Olivia Remie (ed.), *Medieval Iberia: Readings from Christian, Muslim and Jewish Sources*. Philadelphia 1997.

Coomaraswamy, Ananda K., *History of Indian and Indonesian Art*. New York 1985.

Crosby, Alfred W., *Ecological Imperialism: The Biological Expansion of Europe, 900–1900*. Cambridge 1986.

Dalrymple, William, *From the Holy Mountain*. London 1997.

___, *White Moghuls: Love and Betrayal in 18th-century India*. London 2002.

Dante Alighieri, *Die göttliche Komödie: Übersetzt von Karl Witte*. Köln 2005.

Das Gupta, Ashin, *The World of the Indian Ocean Merchant*. New Delhi 2001.

Dihle, Albrecht, *Die Griechen und die Fremden*. München 1994.

Dunning, A. J., *Extremes. Reflections on Human Behaviour*. New York 1992.

Edgerton, Robert, *Sick Societies*. Boston 1992.

Embree, Ainslie T. and Friedrich Wilhelm, *Indien: Geschichte des Subkontinents von der Induskultur bis zum Beginn der englischen Herrschaft*. Frankfurt M. 1969.

Engineer, Asghar Ali, *The Origin and Development of Islam*. Hyderabad 1980.

Euben, Roxanne L., *Enemy in the Mirror. Islamic Fundamentalism and the Limits of Modern Rationalism*. Princeton 1999.

Ferrucci, Franco, *The Poetics of Disguise: The Autobiography of the Work in Homer, Dante, and Shakespeare*. Ithaca 1980.

Finley, M. I., *Aspects of Antiquity*. Harmondsworth 1977.

Fletcher, Richard, *Moorish Spain*. Berkeley 1993.

_____, *The Cross and the Crescent*. London 2003.

Frye, Richard N., *The Golden Age of Persia: The Arabs in the East*. London 2003.

Geertz, Clifford, *The Interpretation of Cultures*. New York 1973.

_____, *Local Knowledge*. New York 2000.

Gerber, Jane S., *The Jews of Spain*. New York 1994.

Ghosh, Amitav, *In an Antique Land*. New Delhi 1992.

Giblin, James Cross, *From Hand to Mouth*. New York 1987.

Glick, Thomas F., *Islamic and Christian Spain in the Early Middle Ages*. Leiden 2005.

Golwalkar, M. S., *We, or Our Nationhood Defined*. Nagpur 1939.

Goody, Jack, *Islam in Europe*. Cambridge 2004.

Goytisolo, Juan, *Kibla: Reisen in die Welt des Islam*. Frankfurt M. 2000.

Greenblatt, Stephen, *Marvellous Possessions*. London 1991.

Haesner, Chhaya, 'A Cultural Diffusion', in *Marg*: Hind and Hellas, Vol. XXXVII, No. 2. Mumbai 1990.

Halliday, Fred, *Islam & the Myth of Confrontation*. London 1996.

Haskins, Charles Homer, *The Renaissance of the Twelfth Century*. Cambridge Mass. 1927.

Henisch, Brigit Anne, *Feast and Fast: Food in Medieval Society*. Philadelphia 1976.

Herodotus, *Histories*. Ware 1996.

Honour, Hugh and John Fleming, *A World History of Art*. London 1991.

Howard, Deborah, *Venice and the East: The Impact of the Islamic World on Venetian Architecture 110–1500*. New Haven 2000.

Hussain, Asaf, *Political Terrorism and the State in the Middle East*. London 1988.

Gabirol, Solomon Ibn, *Selected Poems*. Translated by Peter Cole. Princeton 2001.

Ibn Arabi, *Urwolke und Welt: Mystische Texte des Größten Meisters*. München 2002.

Ibn Tufail, *Hajj ibn Jaqzan der Naturmensch*. Leipzig 1983.

Ibn Tufayl, *Hayy Ibn Yaqzan*. Translated by L. E. Goodman. New York 1972.

Irwin, Robert (ed.), *Night and Horses and the Desert: Classical Arabic Literature*. London 1999.

Jardine, Lisa and Jerry Brotton, *Global Interests: Renaissance Art between East and West*. New York 2000.

Jaeger, Werner, *Early Christianity and Greek Paideia*. Oxford 1961.

Jay, Peter, *Road to Riches or The Wealth of Man*. London 2000.

Kepel, Gilles, *Muslim Extremism in Egypt: The Prophet and the Pharoah*. Translated by Jon Rothschild. Berkeley 1985.

Jayyusi, Salma Khadra (ed.), *The Legacy of Muslim Spain*. 2 vols. New York 1994.

St John of the Cross, *Alchemist of the Soul*. Translated by Antonio T. de Nicolas. York Beach 1989.

Koch, Ebba, *Mughal Architecture*. München 1991.

Kosambi, D. D., *Myth and Reality*. Mumbai 2000.

Kritzeck, James, *Peter the Venerable and Islam*. Princeton 1964.

Kriwaczek, Paul, *In Search of Zarathushtra: The First Prophet and the Ideas That Changed the World*. New York 2003.

Kulke, Eckehard, *The Parsees of India*. München 1974.

Kulke, Hermann and Dietmar Rothermund, *Geschichte Indiens*. München 1998.

Kumar, Amitava, *The Humour and the Pity: On V S Naipaul*. New Delhi 2002.

Lane-Poole, Stanley, *The Muslims in Spain*. New Delhi 2007.

Le Goff, Jacques, *Die Intellektuellen im Mittelalter*, Stuttgart 1991.

Lea, Henry Charles, *The Moriscos of Spain*. Philadelphia 1901.

Lewis, Bernard, *What Went Wrong? The Clash between Islam and Modernity in the Middle East*. London 2002.

Lewis, Joan M., *Religion in Context*. Cambridge 1986.

Lipsitz, George, *Dangerous Crossroads: Popular Music, Postmodernism and the Poetics of Place*. London 1994.

Liu, Xinru, *Ancient India and Ancient China*. New Delhi 1998.

____, *Silk and Religion*. New Delhi 1998.

Maalouf, Amin, *Mörderische Identitäten*. Frankfurt 2000.

Mackintosh-Smith, Tim, *Travels with a Tangerine: A Journey in the Footnotes of Ibn Battutah*. London 2002.

Mann, Vivian B., Thomas F. Glick and Jerrilynn D. Dodds, *Convivencia: Jews, Muslims and Christians in Medieval Spain*. New York 1992.

Mansoor, Ali Yahya, *Die arabische Theorie: Studien zur Entwicklungsgeschichte des abendländischen Minnesangs*. Heidelberg 1966.

Menocal, María Rosa, *The Ornament of the World: How Muslims, Jews and Christians Created a Culture of Tolerance in Medieval Spain*. Boston 2002.

Michell, George, *Hindu Art and Architecture*. London 2000.

Miles, Jack, *God: A Biography*. New York, 1995.

della Mirandola, Pico, *Oration on the Dignity of Man*. Translated by A. Robert Caponigri. Chicago 1956.

Mirza, Hormazdyar, *Outlines of Parsi History, Zoroastrian Religion and Ancient Iranian Art*. Bombay 1999.

Mitter, Partha, *Indian Art*. Oxford 2002.

Nasr, Seyyed Hossein, *Islamic Art and Spirituality*. Delhi 1990.

Noorani, A. G., *The RSS and the BJP: A Division of Labour*. New Delhi 2000.

Peters, F. E., *The Hajj: The Muslim Pilgrimage to Mecca and the Holy Places*. Princeton 1994.

Plotinus, *Enneads*. Translated by S. MacKenna. Harmondsworth 1991.

Prashad, Vijay, *Everybody Was Kung Fu Fighting: Afro-Asian Connections and the Myth of Cultural Purity*. Boston 2002.

Rahman, Syed Azizur, *The Story of Islamic Spain*. New Delhi 2002.

Rahner, Hugo, *Greek Myths and Christian Mystery*. London 1963.

Roberts, Paul William, *Journey of the Magi*. New York 1995.

Rocker, Rudolf, *Nationalismus und Kultur* (2 Bde.). Bremen n.d.

Rolland, Romain, *The Life of Ramakrishna*. Calcutta 1992.

Runciman, Stephen, *A History of the Crusades*. Cambridge 1951.

Russell, Bertrand, *History of Western Philosophy*. London 1966.

Russell, James C., *The Germanization of Early Medieval Christianity*. Oxford 1994.

Ruthven, Malise, *A Fury for God: The Islamist Attack on America*. London 2002.

Sandvoss, Ernst R., *Geschichte der Philosophie*. München 1989.

Schack, Fr. v., *Poesie und Kunst der Araber in Spanien und Sicilien*. Hildesheim 1979.

Schimmel, Annemarie, *Mystische Dimensionen des Islam*. Frankfurt M. 1995.

Schlaffer, Heinz, *Die kurze Geschichte der deutschen Literatur*. München 2002.

Schrott, Raoul Schrott, *Die Erfindung der Poesie*. Frankfurt 1998.

Scott, William Henry, *Looking for the Prehispanic Filipino*. Quezon City 1992.

Shah, Idries, *Learning how to Learn: Psychology and Spirituality in the Sufi Way*. London 1993.

____, *The Sufis*. New York 1971.

Sharma, Jyotirmaya, *Hindutva: Exploring the Idea of Hindu Nationalism*. New Delhi 2003.

____, *Terrifying Vision: Golwalkar, the RSS and India*. New Delhi 2007.

Sikand, Yoginder, *Sacred Spaces: Exploring Traditions of Shared Faith in India*. New Delhi 2003.

Sivan, Emmanuel, *Radical Islam: Mediaeval Theology and Modern Politics*. New Haven 1990.

Skilton, Andrew (Dharmachari Sthiramati), *A Concise History of Buddhism*. Birmingham 1994.

Southern, R. W., *Western Views of Islam in the Middle Ages*. Cambridge 1980.

Stanley, Trevor, *The Quest for Caliphate: Islamist Innovation from Qutb to al-Qaeda*. Melbourne 2003.

Stephans, Condie (trans.), *Fairy Tales of a Parrot*. London/New York n.d.

Strohmaier, Gotthard, *Avicenna*. München 2006.

Subrahmanyam, Sanjay, *The Career and Legend of Vasco da Gama*. Cambridge 1998.

Thapar, Romila, *Interpreting Early India*. New Delhi 1992.

____, *Somanatha: The Many Voices of a History*. New Delhi 2004.

Turner, Howard R., *Science in Medieval Islam*. Austin 1997.

Urvoy, Dominique, *Ibn Rushd: Averroes*. Translated by Olivia Stewart. London 1991.

Varadarajan, Siddharth (ed.), *Gujarat: The Making of a Tragedy*. New Delhi 2002.

de Varthema, Ludovico, *Reisen im Orient*. Sigmaringen 1996.

Voltaire, *Philosophical Dictionary*. Selected and translated by H. I. Woolf. New York 1924.

von Denffer, Ahmad, *Ulum Al-Qur'an: An Introduction to the Sciences of the Quran*. Leicester 1983.

Webster, Jason, *Andalus: Unlocking the Secrets of Moorish Spain*. London 2004.

Wheatcroft, Andrew, *Infidels: A History of the Conflict between Christendom and Islam*. London 2003.

Wink, Andre, *Al-Hind: The Making of the Indo-Islamic World, Vol. I: Early Medieval India and the Expansion of Islam, 7th-11th Centuries*. Leiden 1990.

____, *Al-Hind: The Making of the Indo-Islamic World, Vol. II: The Slave Kings and the Islamic Conquest 11th–13th Centuries*. New Delhi 1999.

Zimmer, Heinrich, *The Philosophies of India*. New York 1951.

____, *Myths and Symbols in Indian Art and Civilization*. New York 1972.

WEBSITES

http://www.brown.edu/Departments/Italian_Studies/pico

http://www.cathares.org

http://etcweb.princeton.edu/dante/pdp/

Index